MW00427335

Sitting with Lao-Tzu

*Discovering the power of the timeless,
the silent, and the invisible in a
clamorous modern world*

ANDREW BEAULAC

Including a New Translation of the *Tao Te Ching*
with attention to the recently discovered *Mawangdui* texts,
and essays explaining key terms and concepts

APOCRYPHILE
PRESS

The Apocryphile Press
1700 Shattuck Ave. #81
Berkeley, CA 94709
www.apocryphile.org

Sitting with Lao Tzu
ISBN 978-1-944769-41-3

Printed in the United States of America

Please join our mailing list at
www.apocryphilepress.com/free
and we'll keep you up-to-date on all our new releases
—and we'll also send you a FREE BOOK.

Visit us today!

Dedication

For Philip and Lindsay

We might call this world the forms of the Formless,
the shapes of what has no substance.
It is described as obscure and elusive.
Seeking to encounter it there is nowhere to begin,
and to follow it there is nowhere we must go.
Just hold fast to the timeless Way
in order to manage what is present now,
and thus penetrate the ancient origin.
This present moment is the continuing thread of the Universal Way.

LAO-TZU

Acknowledgments

It is with deep gratitude that I thank Red Pine for his generosity of time and expertise in helping me work through questions about the translation, for reading the essays and making helpful comments, and for his encouragement to go on with the work and seek publication. My heartfelt thanks to Sarah Cassatt for always having a ready ear and interested mind when I went on about the Tao and Lao-tzu, and for reading through the manuscript with a careful eye and listing so many helpful suggestions, all of which I have followed. I thank Mark Ambrose for countless long phone discussions about the Tao as we enjoyed "solving the world's problems" with its timeless wisdom, regardless of whether the world would listen. Finally, I thank Pat Sullivan for proofreading with such a careful eye, finding so many typos and errors to which I had become "snow-blind" from looking at the manuscript for too long. Any remaining errors are, of course, no one's responsibility but my own.

Contents

About the Translation

Many venerable translations began in the nineteenth century, when Chinese was rendered into English under the Wade-Giles system of Romanization. This has been carried on for works from Chinese antiquity, and you see it in the terms *Tao Te Ching, Lao-tzu, Chuang-tzu,* and others. I took the advice of the publisher in retaining "Lao-tzu" and "Tao-Te-Ching" for the book's title because of their name-recognition; interested people are *looking for* those words. Within the book, however, I have chosen to render Chinese terms with the current Pinyin Romanization because 1) it has been the international standard since 1982, and 2) its suggested pronunciations are a little less bizarre than many from the Wade-Giles system. For clarification, I usually follow the first Pinyin transliteration of a Chinese term with the Wade-Giles version in parentheses. For example: *Laozi* (*Lao-tzu*), or *ziran* (*tzu-jan*). Though neither system provides a perfect pronunciation of the Chinese, *ziran* is much closer than *tzu-jan*!

Because of the many differences in various translations, I wanted to understand what Chinese words and concepts lay behind such varied translations. I had begun unpacking the Laozi book using the Wang Pi and Ho-shang Kung commentaries provided by Alan K.L. Chan. In addition, I scrutinized a word-by-word Chinese text listing many possible definitions for each character, and various grammatical and interpretive notes. Also, I relied heavily on Red Pine's wonderful work which includes indispensable commentaries by Chinese Daoists from the last two-thousand years. Even giving the text due diligence, I nevertheless needed some sound guidance for certain parts, and verification that my understanding of Daoist thought as expressed in the essays was reasonably accurate.

Some years ago, it was my good fortune to and great pleasure to sit with Red Pine, one of the foremost translators of old Chinese Daoist and Buddhist texts. He happened to live within traveling distance and, more importantly, he was so generous with his time that he invited me to his home to work through problematic parts of the Chinese texts. He also read through my preliminary essays and made helpful suggestions. My deepest thanks to this kind and generous scholar.

More often than not, being accurate and literal with a Chinese text and making it communicate well in English are mutually exclusive options, and I was vacillating endlessly between the two. What I *wanted* to do was translate the heart-mind of the Laozi text for the modern western mind, which is so very different. Many times an accurate word-for-word literal translation of the text will leave a western reader shrugging with indifference or incomprehension. Over cups of the best Oolong tea I have ever tasted, Red Pine told me the most important thing for my work, which, as I remember it, was basically: "Translation is like a dance; if you and Laozi are hearing the same melody, you will be dancing in unison even of you are on the other side of the room from each other. You don't need to stand on Laozi's toes in your translation." I was immediately released from a wooden, word-for-word translation.

The purpose of this book is not to provide yet another translation of this profound text. The *Dao De Jing* is already the second or third most translated book in the world! I own fifteen different English translations. Why create another? For *Sitting with Lao-tzu*, I might have chosen one to quote with permission, but my favorite renderings of various verses were from too many contrasting translations. I had to get at the Chinese text behind them all, and see what is actually there. Then various principles of analysis and interpretation were employed which led to a fresh translation.

Such a long and intricate journey is its own reward. So, even though this translation began as incidental to the essays, it has become essential: I feel it gives a number of obscure passages a clarity lacking in many translations and helps bridge the heart of Laozi to the modern western mind. I hope readers will discover in it a faithful conveyance of the Laozi's *mind behind the words*.

The *Dao* is what is subtly underlying all creation. As such, it is prior to, and quite beyond, all words and descriptions. But it is also treated as a life-path, a *Way*. In most verses I leave it untranslated, as *Dao*, but not always. Anytime you see the capitalized *Way*, it is a translation of the same word: *Dao*.

The essays are preparatory to the translation, because they explain important words and concepts the reader will encounter. Nevertheless, I feel that one's initial exposure should be to Laozi first, and so begin with the translation of the eighty-one verses. Readers are encouraged to approach this book in whichever order they prefer. Within the translation also, some verses are given explanations of textual interpretive choices, cultural context, or thoughts for meditative reflection.

When I first encountered Laozi, I was stunned by how contrary it is to almost everything I had been conditioned to think and feel. Later, I was amused by how honest, natural and obvious it is. Sitting with Laozi yourself, your mind may become quiet as you discover a timeless consciousness. One of Laozi's successors, Zhuangzi (or Chuang-tzu), describes the journey thus:

> Imagine that we are wandering in the palace of No-Particular-Place. Our great theme is the harmonious unity that is timeless and never fails. Join with me in the effortless action, in simplicity and quietude, in non-attachment and clarity, in harmony and ease.

> Now my intentions are aimless – I hold to no destination, and arrive holding no ideas about arriving. When I come or go, there is no purpose behind it: I was there, now I am here, and I will not recognize an end of this journey. I wander and rest in limitless vastness.

Preface

The title of this book, *Sitting With Lao-tzu*, is a reference to countless early mornings and late evenings sitting quietly with an ancient text called the *Tao Te Ching* (or Classic Text of the Way and its Power). I often imagined I was in the presence of its legendary author, Laozi (or Lao-tzu, and pronounced something close to *Lau-dzuh*), a wise old mystic from the sixth century BCE.[1] Regardless of whether he was the actual author, one author among others, or even a historical figure, Laozi has, for me, assumed the role of a wise old friend, a great-grandfatherly figure who makes plain the hidden realities of life, and shows how to flow with supreme effectiveness. He is a spiritual mentor, an ancient friend, a guide, an immortal with a knowing smile. But the wisdom of the Laozi book is too often obscured in the West by our unfamiliarity with an Asian conceptual world, especially one that is twenty-five centuries old! The essays following the eighty-one verses of Laozi's work seek to bridge his world with our very different modern conceptual world.

This book is about a way of return to one's own true life. In any society, ancient or modern, which has made busyness a virtue, lost itself in pursuing the accumulation of power, knowledge, and material goods, and finds its only way forward to be into increasing complexity and a one-sided quest for incessant growth, people find their lives displaced, and long for a return to authenticity, freedom, and simplicity. Returning to one's true life is returning to pure *being-ness*. These essays will introduce anyone newly exposed to Laozi to a wisdom that

---

1   The *Dao De Jing* is usually assumed to be a body of wisdom collected from the sixth through the fourth centuries B.C.E. rather than the product of Laozi alone.

we already know at our deepest level, but seem to have forgotten on the turbulent and distracted level of everyday living.

My hope is that readers find not just inspirational reflections but a universe in which freedom and harmony flow as its natural current. This book is about the possibility of living without conflict, whether internal or external. For some, Laozi's wisdom might be laughed off as the political and mystical musings of a thoughtful but impractical old man. As a man of Dao (Tao), he is an oddball who finds no virtue in busyness for its own sake, and sees striving too hard at improving things as meddlesome, tiring, unnatural, and ultimately counterproductive. He finds no true strength in rigidity because inflexible things are brittle. What can bow or bend can remain whole. Likewise, force is unnatural, convulsive, and leads to crumbling results. Further, he sees erudition as a chief cause of restlessness and dissatisfaction, and the over-accumulation of material goods as keeping us from simplicity, freedom, and true satisfaction. A person of Dao sees extravagance and excess as undesirable as rotting leftovers, or extraneous growths on the body.

Laozi's treasures are compassion, economy of life, and humility. He prefers the dim and quiet to the glaring and noisy. His call is to a return from over-complexity to a simplicity in touch with what is real in itself, from the contrived to the spontaneous, from artifice to naturalness, from separation to reconnection with life and the natural world. He calls for life attuned to the Universal rather than the transitory.

Is the Dao relevant to us?

The history of Western civilization is largely a story that has imagined progress to be a linear, "ever onward and upward" journey. This is certainly true of technological advancement, politics, and economics. Political power looks perpetually *outward* for an ever increasing persuasion of the masses to particular points of view in order to expand the borders of its economy and ideology. One finds little evidence that politics spends time looking *inward*, that is, giving as much thought to self-correction, or re-evaluating its own validity as the world evolves.

Economics is another other force in the world reaching ever outward for more and more resources to exploit and convert to material wealth, too often treating other humans as exploitable resources. Presumably, it is not the job of politics, economics, or technology to look inward. Wisdom, on the other hand *is* inward, valuing self-correction, reevaluation, and reflection. In the west such practices are relegated to the domains of psychology, spirituality, or religion, and are considered private matters with no sure application in the larger public scale. Thus, the present situations in our economies, politics, compromised health, and global environmental devastation demonstrate the problems that arise when purely outward-looking "progress" and technology are unmoderated by wisdom. Also, these problems are but the symptoms of a faulty world-view.

That technology could be "inward looking" is not as nonsensical as it might at first seem. It simply means, for example, that in developing the technological *ability* to genetically modify people or make nuclear weapons, we might also develop of a degree of wisdom commensurate with such potentials, and question whether the human race really should go that route, or whether it will be possible to keep such technologies away from the ambitions of fools.

If politics looked inward, it might ask how it wants to relate to the rest of the world. Must political interactions imply competition and conflict, or can they express an honest interest in mutual benefit? Lacking any return to the inward aspect, a political world will seek to move "ever onward and upward" for some end regardless of how harmful the means. We watch honesty give way to political expediency while public information is replaced by "spin," a euphemism for cultural deceit and propaganda. Careful thought loses its position, and we have actually come to accept that politicians do whatever is best for their own careers, regardless of whether it is best for the citizens. Consequently, there is now a chasm between how we may feel about life in our inward or personal selves and the view of life we are supposed to accept as necessary according to our ever outward looking, non-contemplative institutions.

So, we have to wonder: Can the Laozi book be at all relevant today, apart from private spirituality? People longing for naturalness and reconnection tend to find in the *Dao De Jing* one of the wisest treatises ever written. Surprisingly, it presents no rules or lists of things one must do. It presents no plan for a utopian dream or even personal goals. Rather, it presents a view of life – of the Universe and the world and humanity's place in it – as one unified field in which striving and struggling make no sense and are even counterproductive. Here is a wisdom that comes from observing both the natural world and our constructed societies, and suggests that the human propensity for controlling things leads ultimately to an unsustainable or unhealthy result. It relieves us of the burdensome illusion that only perpetual increase is good, and it allows us to be at peace with the ebb as well as the flow of life. It shows how the uses of force, dominion and control lead to an ever anxious view of the world, and reflect our ignorance of Nature's processes.

There are many good introductions to the text and to Laozi, and it is not the purpose of this book repeat them. For those who find themselves interested, I heartily recommend four that stand out above the rest as being detailed, relevant, and thoughtful, namely, those of Wing-tsit Chan, D.C. Lau, Robert G. Henricks, and Red Pine, whose books are listed in the bibliography.

dao de jing

The *Dao De Jing* of Laozi

1

We can speak about the Dao, but the eternal Dao is beyond words;
we can give it a name, but names and concepts are not eternal.
Nameless, is the maiden-like source of heaven and earth;
naming it, we find the mother of all the myriad things.
When concepts cease, one perceives a hidden essence;
clinging to concepts one perceives ten-thousand things.

The hidden essence and the ten-thousand things
arise from the same Source, but are distinguished by naming.
This is the primal mystery –
the Origin hidden beneath all origins –
the gateway to everything's mysterious essence.

Notes: In line 3 "the maiden-like source" is actually just *shi*, usually meaning "beginning." But according to the *Shuowen* (a second-century etymological dictionary) *shi* means "a virgin," (see Red Pine, p. 3)

17

and is thus what is prior to being "the mother" in the following line. The fullness of all the myriad phenomena come from the primordial emptiness of "the nameless." The mystery of the existence of the universe is in these two aspects:

1) the Primal Source, which is itself unborn, eternal, timeless, beyond causes or conditions, and thus unnameable, maiden-like, a subtle, hidden essence, as unmanifested pure potential, and

2) the manifest "ten-thousand things," birthed, impermanent, claimed by time, conditional, differentiated through naming.

The temporal, finite, limited, manifest world is secretly *one with* the eternal, infinite, limitless, unmanifested pure potential. As we encounter the Nameless, the particular and the universal are realized as inseparable. The infinite ground of Being is the hidden side of the finite world. This is the mystery beyond mysteries, the gateway to understanding everything.

The 3rd and 4th lines may be punctuated differently, so their translation becomes: "Emptiness is the origin of heaven and earth; "Existence" is the mother of all the myriad things."

In line 5 "Emptied of preconceptions" is simply *wú yù*, "without desires," but *yù* also has to do with deep-seated thought constructs or mental patterns. The clinging, egoistic mind is attached to perceptions of matter and its divergences, that is, to forms and names. A quiet, non-clinging mind perceives the hidden essence underlying all things.

2

Perceiving some things as beautiful
requires the concept of "ugly."
Perceiving some things as good
requires the concept of "bad."
Likewise,
    being and non-being require each other;
    difficult and easy perfect each other;
    long and short define each other;
    high and low depend on each other;
    it takes tones and intervals to make a melody;
    front and back assume each other.

This is why the sage:
    does not force things in daily affairs
    and does not use words to convey her teaching.
    The myriad things arise though she doesn't begin them.
    She acts, but without expectations,
    achieves, but without dwelling on it.
The sage finds no reason to cling, and yet nothing is lost.

Note: The pairs of opposites (being/non-being, difficult/easy, long/
short, high/low, tones/intervals, front/back) recall the two sides of
the yin/yang symbol: they are polarities within the same circle and
each has its heart in the center of its opposite, signifying that they
arise mutually. Like activity and rest, they balance each other. What
we perceive as sound is actually a vibration of sound and silence,
and light is actually wavelengths of light and dark. Light is not good
nor dark bad. We can cease striving to accentuate the positive or to
eliminate the negative.

3

If you don't honor some as superior, people will cease to contend.
If you don't place value on what is hard to obtain, people will not
become thieves.
If you don't show off possessions, people's hearts will not become
unsettled.

So, this is how a sage governs:
He empties people's minds and fills their bellies.
He weakens their ambitions and strengthens their bones.
If he can keep people innocent of knowledge and attachments,
and those with knowledge from daring to act,
there will be no disorder.

Note: Emptying people's minds (line 5) and keeping them innocent
of knowledge (line 7) is not a petition for ignorance. The mind too
full of ideas about striving for superiority, gaining what is hard to
come by, and the status of possessions needs to be pacified by being
emptied of such delusions. "Filling bellies" represents satisfaction
with the basic necessities of life. But there is also in Daoist thought
a de-emphasis of Confucian educational refinement, where schol-
arly learning was a means of competition for status as a superior
or worthy one. Zhuangzi tells a story personifying *Wei-wuwei* (the
action of non-action) as a character who says, "Not knowing is profound; knowing is shallow: to be without knowledge is to be inward,
to know is to be outward." The psyche that perpetually leaves its
center to reach outward is ambitious (line 6) to make its mark on
the world, and causes the disorder mentioned in the final line.

4

The Dao is empty.
But used, it proves inexhaustible!
It is deep beyond measure,
the Ancestor preceding all the myriad things.
With Dao, sharp edges are blunted,
    complications are unraveled,
    harsh light is softened,
    even dust settles into place.
So still and clear, it seems barely present.
I do not know from whom it could have come;
it seems to have preceded even *Di*, the lord of creation.

5

Heaven and earth don't show favoritism;
they treat the myriad things dispassionately, like straw dogs.
Accordingly, the sage is without preference,
and treats everyone dispassionately.
The space between Heaven and Earth is like a bellows,
　　that is, an emptiness that never fails to supply,
　　and the more it works, the more it brings forth.
　　But the chattering away of learned ideas is tiresome;
　　it's better to remain centered within.

Note: Straw dogs could be used ceremonially by a shaman for events such as summoning rain. A straw dog was first decorated, and afterward discarded, but neither action was a measure of love or hate. In the same way, Heaven and earth do not love or hate those who come and go. The sage, too, treats all people alike, not loving some and hating others. In the final sentence, the Chinese text seems to have a humorous contrast between the helpful blowing of air from a bellows and the tiresome blowing air of too much speech! Save your breath and remain centered.

6

The spirit that is like a valley never dies;
and is called "the mysterious feminine."
The opening of this mysterious feminine
is the root of Heaven and earth.
It shows just the subtlest hint of existence,
yet, utilizing it, you find it inexhaustible.

Note: A valley is a place of fruitfulness and growth because it is a place of confluence; it is the low place which passively receives water, soils, seeds, and life energy from its surroundings. Likewise, the "valley spirit" of the unassuming sage is fruitful through passivity. Mingling heaven and earth, the sage operates by the inexhaustible Dao. Compare verse 8.

7

Heaven is everlasting and Earth is ancient.
The reason Heaven and Earth endure so
is that they don't exist for themselves.
Likewise, the sage always goes last yet ends up in front,
is not self-concerned yet is always preserved.
Empty of self-interest, one's interests are realized.

8

The highest goodness is like water
which benefits all things, contends with none,
and flows into the low places that others disdain.
In this, water resembles the Dao.
> In dwelling, what matters is the land.
> In thinking, what matters is depth.
> In relations with others, what matters is taking Heaven's view.
> In speaking, what matters is sincerity.
> In leadership, what matters is harmonious order.
> In work, what matters is efficiency.
> In action, what matters is the right moment.

Follow the Way that never contends and you will be without fault.

9

Grasping a cup and overfilling
is not as good as stopping in time!
If you over-sharpen a blade,
it will dull more quickly.
If you fill a place with gold and jade,
no one can make it safe.
If opulence and rank make you important,
you have begun your own downfall.
Be content to complete your task and step away from it.
This is the way of Heaven.

10

In cultivating your bodily soul to embrace the One,
can you abide there, undivided?
In attending to your vital breath and returning to suppleness,
can you attain the suppleness of a newborn?
In cleansing your inner mirror
can you leave no residue?
In serving people and governing the state
can you avoid the cunning of expertise?
Within activity and stillness
can you hold to the role of the female?
Even with discernment penetrating the four directions
can you renounce knowing?

Giving life and nurturing –
giving life, yet without possessing,
tending to people without ruling–
these describe true virtue.

Note: "Within activity and stillness..." is *tian men qi he*, or "heaven's gate opening, closing." According to Wang Pi, the gate of heaven simply means the way of Nature. Wang-An-Shih (1021-1086) says Heaven's Gate is the gate through which all creatures enter and leave (see Pine, p. 21), which sounds like a reference to birth and death. But this verse appears to be about abiding in Dao both in meditative stillness and during engagement in activity. "Opening" refers to activity, which is the male principle, and "closing" to stillness, or the female principle. The "opening and closing" could thus refer to Nature's vicissitudes such as the coming and going of things, or activity and rest. Line 10 asks whether we can remain in the female principle, which means staying centered in stillness (and yogic connection with Dao), no matter what may come. Interestingly, Kuo Hsiang (d. 312) says the gate of Heaven is the same as verse 1's gateway to everything's hidden essence.

11

Thirty spokes unite on a hub
and yet it's the hole at the center that makes a wheel usable.
Clay is fashioned into a vessel
and its inner emptiness makes the vessel useful.
Doors and windows are cut into a house
and empty spaces make a house livable.
Sure, tangible things mark gain,
but emptiness is the essential.

12

The five colors dim one's eyes.
The five musical notes deaden one's ears.
The five tastes dull one's palate.
Too much chasing and hunting maddens the mind.
Treasured accumulations impede one's movement.
Thus, the sage is concerned with the inner,
and not with what the eyes see.
He rejects "that out there" and holds to "this in here."

Note: The five colors were blue, yellow, white, black, and red. Associated with each were the five tones, five tastes, and five elements of the material world. The thought here is that our focus on sensory stimulation overrides communion with the hidden essence that underlies all the varied phenomena. Then, chasing after sensory things, the mind loses track of what is real. What the sage knows is not gained through sensory stimulation; it is discovered in quiet centeredness.

13

"Favor and disgrace: both are sources of anxiety."
"Regard great affliction as a bodily matter."

What does it mean, "Favor and disgrace: both are sources of anxiety"?
Favor wanes, so gaining it brings anxiety about losing it.
That is why both favor and disgrace are sources of anxiety.

What does it mean, "Regard great affliction as a bodily matter"?
I can only have great affliction when I think I am this body.
When I have realized I am not this body, what affliction do I bear?
Try regarding the entire world as your body;
then you may be fit to be entrusted with the world.
Do so in love, and you are fit to be a leader in the world.

Note: "I can only have great affliction when I think I am this body."
If you are *not* the body, then the real "you" is the subtle or hidden
essence underlying *all* things (verse 1, notes), including your
body and mind. Identified with the finite, conditioned, temporary
body-mind, one experiences anxiety and afflictions. Observing
the body and mind from a deeper level, the perceiver cannnot
be also the perceived. Centered in the stillness of the Dao, one
observes all that comes and goes (bodily changes, thoughts and
feelings arising and disappearing), but is not identified with them.
Instead, one's true identity is the changeless Dao. Understanding
and practicing this is a matter of yogic cultivation. Adapting verse
1, we could say, "when identification with the body-mind ceases,
one perceives one's true essence; identified with body-mind one
perceives a separate self."

14

Looking for it, we see nothing and call it invisible.
Listening, we hear nothing and call it inaudible.
Grasping, there is nothing to get hold of and we call it intangible.
Such qualities are beyond scrutiny and definitions –
"invisible," "inaudible," and "intangible" all dissolve into oneness.

This oneness is the One–
in which there is no high and bright aspect,
versus some low and dark part aspect.
Reaching outward the One is limitless;
rebounding, it returns to non-existence.
So really this world could be called the forms of the Formless,
the shapes of what has no substance.
This is why the *Dao* is called "obscure" and "elusive."

Seeking it, we begin nowhere but here;
following it, there is nowhere we must go.
Holding fast to the timeless Way
you succeed in what is already present.
Doing so you penetrate the ancient origin, and realize that
this present moment is the continuing thread of the Universal Way.

15

The ancient masters, skilled at cultivating Dao,
discerned the hidden essence and penetrated its mystery.
Their depth could not be fathomed.
Because they were unfathomable,
we resort to such descriptions as:
>very deliberate, as if crossing a stream in winter,
>very alert, as if watching all directions,
>so reverent, as if only a visitor here,
>as unconcerned with self as melting ice,
>solid and uncontrived as uncarved wood,
>vast and open as a valley,
>refusing differentiation, like muddy water.

Muddied water becomes clear again through stillness.
So also the best actions arise from stillness and clarity.
One who holds to the Way does not long for constant filling.
Not longing to be filled, one can grow old unconcerned with renewal
or completion.

16

Realize emptiness as the utmost
and maintain tranquility as your center.
The ten-thousand things arise mutually,
and accordingly, return to their one Source.
Truly, everything emerges and, after growing, returns to its root.
Returning to our Root is tranquil stillness;
it is the tranquility of returning to one's true nature.
Returning to one's true nature means tuning in to the changeless.
Tuning in to the changeless is enlightenment.
Not knowing the changeless is the delusion which creates misery.

Knowing the changeless makes one all-embracing.
　　To be all-embracing is to be unprejudiced.
　　To be unprejudiced is to be truly noble.
　　To be noble is to be of Heaven.
　　To be of Heaven is to be in accord with the Dao.
　　To be in accord with the Dao means to live long, free of peril.

Note: "Tuning in to the changeless" is *zhi chang*, and could also be
translated as "being attuned to the eternal," or "knowing that which
lasts." *Chang*, here and in verse 1, I have rendered as "changeless" to
convey not just something enduring, but *timeless*. It is that which is
unborn and never dies, that which is uncreated, unconditioned –
that which is beyond causes and conditions.

17

With the best rulers the people are barely aware of their presence.
Next best are those who are loved and praised.
Worse are leaders who are feared.
The worst are leaders who are despised –
faithless leaders complain that no one is faithful!

The best ruler remains unassertive, and is not prone to speeches.
When he completes his task, the people say, "*We* did it, naturally."

18

When the Great Way is abandoned,
policies for benevolence and morality are instituted.
When knowledge and cleverness appear,
great hypocrisy and pretense follow in their wake.
It is when families lose their natural harmony,
that family respect and love are touted.
Finally, it is when the nation is in darkness and strife
that we hear of patriotic officials.

19

Be rid of holiness; throw out learning,
and people will benefit a hundred times over.
Be rid of benevolence; throw out morality,
and people will rediscover respect and love.
Be rid of ingenuity; throw out profit-seeking,
and thieves and crooks will disappear.
Those three principles are just the externals, thus, insufficient.
So, let us abide in these inward three:

Recognizing what is genuine, you embrace your original simplicity.

Dropping self-interest, you curb habituation.

Emptying yourself of enculturation, you end anxiety.

20

What little difference there is between "yea" and "nay."
"Good" and "bad" – can you really define the difference?
Am I supposed to worry about all the distinctions others make?
If I do, there is no end to worry!

Before their moon has waxed to its full limit
everybody is very happy like they are partaking at a great feast
or climbing to the sightseeing platform in springtime.
Alone, I remain unmoving, showing no signs,
an infant who hasn't yet smiled.
I am a drifter in this world claiming no particular place as home.
Most people have plenty to spare; I remain deficient, a fool, a simpleton!
Worldly people want to be dazzlingly bright; I alone seem dim.
Worldly people make clear distinctions; I alone lack their certainties.
I drift with the current, blow with the winds, anchorless!
Most people have purpose-driven lives, but I am untrainable and unrefined.
This is why I'm different from others:
    I live by the nourishment of the Great Mother.

21

The actions of real virtue and real effectiveness
are drawn from the Dao alone.
How is it that the Dao becomes a Universe of things?
The Dao's becoming any manifest thing is blurred and elusive;
Blurred and elusive, it nevertheless contains images of form.
Elusive and indistinct, but from its core matter arises.
Secret and obscure!
Yet in it is the vital force.
This vital force is quite genuine;
its evidence is in everything.
That is why, from this moment back to ancient times,
its manifesting has never ceased.
So, follow that from which everything comes.
How do we recognize that from which everything comes?
Through everything as it is right now.

Notes: In textual analysis, the earliest texts are usually preferred, but sometimes a later change is a correction or clarification. The early Mawangdui texts have for line 2 *Dao zhi wu*, which would mean, simply, "the Dao as a thing" ["...is blurred and elusive"]. Later texts supply an extra word: *Dao zhi wei wu* which gives line 2 the sense of "As for the Dao becoming a thing..." and thus introduces the mystery of emptiness becoming the fullness of physical cosmos. I agree with Henricks that the later addition of *wei* is likely a correction where the earlier text was missing a word, as this verse as a whole is made up mostly of four-character lines. Further, the addition of *wei* makes good sense contextually for the discussion which follows it: "As for the Dao becoming a thing..." introduces the question of how it is that Dao, which is empty and formless, becomes a world of tangible forms, or things.

In lines 4, 5, and 7, "blurred" (*huang*, meaning indistinct or unclear) is, in the Mawangdui texts, *wang*, in which Red Pine sees the image of a full moon, and thus renders the line "waxes and wanes." This moon imagery also makes sense in the context of fullness and emptiness. The point is that if the Dao acts in the world by emptiness and yet nothing is lacking, so too the efficacy of a person of Dao comes from the place of emptiness yet will find nothing will be lacking.

"Matter" in line 9 translates *wu*, (the same *wu* of "the ten-thousand things") and has to do with substance, and all the distinguishable objects of physical reality.

22

Bend so you remain whole.
Bow, and be lifted upright.
Be empty so you may be filled.
Expend energy and you will be renewed.
Have little and you will gain.
But have too much and you just become confused.

The sages hold to the One and are like shepherds for all below
Heaven:
Not standing in their own light they shine clearly.
Not self-righteous they are respected.
Not boasting they have merit.
Not self-approving they lead.
Competing with no one, no one can compete with them.
When the ancients said, "Bend so you remain whole"
These were not just idle words.
True wholeness is in returning.

23

To be of few and quiet words is to be natural:
    high winds don't blow all morning,
    and heavy rains don't last all day.
What produces these?
Heaven and earth.
If Heaven and earth do not persist,
    how much less the works of man.
So, in daily life,
    one devoted to the Way becomes one with the Way;
    one devoted to its power becomes one with its power;
    one devoted to loss becomes one with loss.

To one identified with Dao, the Dao is happy to receive him.
To one identified with its power, its power is happy to receive him.
To one identified with living without Dao, the Dao is happy to let him go.

24

Lifted on tiptoes, one cannot stand firm.
With too big a stride, one cannot walk far.
One who flaunts himself does not really shine.
One who is self-approving is not really superior.
Boasting about oneself reveals no actual merit.
One who is self-important does not endure.

From the perspective of the Way,
these are like rotting leftovers to be thrown out, or useless activity.
In nature, creatures avoid such waste.
A person of the Way does not live like that.

25

There is something – undifferentiated and permeating all things –
that existed before Heaven and earth.
It is silent! A bodiless vastness!
It alone stands unchanging
and can be considered the Mother of the Universe.
I am unable to name the Nameless,
so I nick-name it *Dao*.
If I had to give it a name, I'd call it "Great."
"Great," means it reaches everywhere,
cycling to the farthest out things,
and back again to the source.
So,

the Dao is great,
Heaven is great,
Earth is great,
and the ruler is also great.

The ruler must take his place within this order:

Humanity follows Earth,
Earth follows Heaven,
Heaven follows the Dao,
and the Dao is what is of itself so.

26

> The weighty is root of the light;
> and the serene is ruler of the restless.
> Just so, a noble person may travel all day
> and not leave behind his supplies.

In his protected camp he is at ease and unconcerned.
Would a king over ten thousand chariots take *himself* more lightly than he does the empire?

> Frivolous actions stray from the Source;
> Restlessness strays from self-mastery.

27

> The true journey leaves neither tracks nor trace.
> True speech is beyond fault or fault-finding.
> True reckoning requires neither math nor record-keeping.
> True shutting needs neither bolt nor bar, yet cannot be opened.
> True binding requires neither rope nor twine, yet cannot be undone.

This is the level of skill a sage uses in saving people;
He rejects no one, nothing useful is abandoned.
This is called following one's light.
In such practice, the good person is simply a teacher,
and the bad person is the good person's raw material.
But without honoring the teacher as such
or caring for the raw material as such,
any learning is great confusion.
This is seeing through to the essence.

28

Know the masculine but hold to the feminine
and be like a river-valley in the world.
Acting as a river-valley in the world
the eternal virtue does not depart from you.
When the eternal virtue does not depart from you,
you become again as a newborn child.
Know the bright but hold to the dim
and be an example for the world.
Acting as an example for the world
you won't stray from the eternal virtue.
Not straying from the eternal virtue
you return to the limitless.

Know the glorious but hold to the lowly
and be the world's valley.
Acting as the world's valley
you find sufficiency in the eternal virtue,
and so return to being like uncarved wood.
After all, the original wood is split
only to be carved into mere tools.
For a sage, such are the chief officials.
A master tailor does not create a lot of cut up pieces;
a great ruler does not split things unnaturally.

Notes: The uncarved wood is a picturesque way of expressing *pu*, which refers to one's natural state, original simplicity, genuineness, or purity. In this verse John C.H. Wu translates it as "Primal Simplicity." This is contrasted with *san*, which has to do with splitting, separating, breaking up, or carving, which is seen as artificiality. The sage values the natural state of wood over ornately carved tools. The chief officials were often overly ornate, but mere tools, having been separated from their primal, natural state.

In the second section, "Not straying from the eternal virtue you return to the limitless," the limitless here is *wu-ji*, which, being overly literal, means "no ridge-pole." It refers to the Dao prior to creation, the empty Dao that produces the beginning (see the notes on verse 42). The primordial *wu-ji* is the ultimate, the boundless, or infinite. "Not straying from the eternal virtue (*de*) is acting from the Dao alone, or letting yourself act solely as the outworking virtue of Dao. Not straying from this, you return to infinity.

The last two lines are actually only one in the text, which may be translated with either sense, and I wanted to give both.

29

Some think they can manage the world through control,
but I perceive no successful end to this.
The world is the vessel of the Sacred
and is not to be shoved around!
Acting upon it only ruins it.
Seizing it, you lose it!

For all beings there are:
    times to follow and times to lead,
    times to breathe gently and times to breathe hard,
    times of overcoming and times of succumbing.
This is why the sage rejects extremes, excess, and extravagance.

30

Anyone who assists a ruler in harmony with the Way
does not make use of military might.
That way of acting usually comes back at you.
The places occupied by armies grow brambles and barbs,
and the aftermath of great war is great misfortune and lean years.
The skillful commander wins, but knows when to stop.
He does not venture a path of domination.
He wins, but does not glory in it;
wins, but does not swagger or gloat;
wins, but never dominates.

> Pushing anything to its utmost only exhausts it,
> and thus goes against the Way.
> What goes against the Way soon comes to its own end.

31

Truly, great weapons are tools of great misfortune;
and are loathsome to all creatures.
The person of the Way does not live by them.

In peaceful times a wise ruler honors the left
and only in war honors the right.
Thus, weapons are not the tools of a wise ruler,
but are tools of grave misfortune –
he uses them only when there's no other choice.
His highest priority is dispassion and calm,
and if he must subdue, he takes no delight in warfare.
To enjoy victory is to enjoy killing people.
Truly, one who enjoys killing will never be satisfied in this world!
On happy occasions we honor the left;
and on sorrowful occasions we honor the right.
The second in command stands on the left; the commander on the right.
In this we see that a military ceremony is conducted like a funeral.
You can only kill multitudes with anguish and weeping,
so observe a victory as you would a funeral.

Note: Only one who abhors slaughtering people is fit to rule and unite a nation. For Laozi, weapons are nothing but instruments of evil. Only those who feel disconnected from nature and other people can glory in using them. The verse nevertheless recognizes there may be times when there is no other choice but to engage in battle. But as in the preceding verse, victories are treated as a tragic, if necessary, measure. A ruler in harmony with the Dao knows when to stop, and does not follow victories with domination or oppression.

32

The Way is forever nameless.
Though it is both elementary and infinitesimal,
no one in the world has power over it.
If princes and kings could hold to it,
all things would yield of their own accord.
The harmonizing of Heaven and earth
causes a sweet dew to fall on all people alike;
peace and harmony ensue not by any decree, but spontaneously.
As soon as there are regulations things need to be named.
Now that they are named, it's time to stop dividing.
Knowing when to stop, you avoid danger.

If you want to understand the Dao in this world, picture this:
    many rivulets flowing into streams,
    streams flowing into great rivers,
    and great rivers flowing into the one ocean.

33

Understanding others is knowledge,
but understanding oneself is enlightenment.
Conquering others is merely force;
conquering oneself is true strength.

Knowing what is enough is wealth.
Making right effort shows inner resolve.
Holding to one's center, one endures.
Dying with these intact, one is immortal.

34

The great Way indeed flows like water –
sometimes left, sometimes right.
It succeeds in its tasks without making a name for itself.
It enfolds and nourishes all things and claims no dominion.
Ever ambitionless, it could be called "small."
But it is the home to which everything returns.
Thus, even claiming no dominion, it is called "Great."
Never acting as a great one, greatness is realized.

35

    Hold to the Great Image
    and the world will come to you –
    come, and not be harmed –
    and will enjoy harmony and health.

For music and pastries even passing folk will stop,
but words about the Way seem plain and flavorless.
This is because looked for, it can't even be seen,
and listened for, it can't even be heard,
but utilized, it is inexhaustible!

Note: The Great Image is the Great Dao. It is called an image because it is formless and empty. Yet it is that from which all physical forms come. When one is in harmony with the Great (or Primal) Image, other creatures recognize a harmonious spirit, and come without fear of harm. There are Daoist and Buddhist stories of sages who lived in harmony with wild beasts. The Zen sage Feng-kan ("Big Stick"), a friend of the ninth-century poet Han-shan (Cold Mountain), was said to have come out of the mountains to enter the Temple's front gate riding on the back of a tiger! He was in harmony with the Great Image.

36

If you want to decrease something,
bring it to the limit of its expansion.
If you want to weaken something,
bring it to the limit of its strength.
If you want to topple something,
bring it to the limit of its height.
What you would deprive,
bring to the limit of its enrichment.
This is called obscure wisdom;
it's how the soft and yielding conquers the hard and strong.
As a fish pulled from its depths doesn't survive,
so weapons of the State should never need to surface.

Note: In the ninth line, "This is called obscure wisdom" is a recurring phrase: *shi wei wei ming*. The *wei* of the ending phrase *wei ming* has a pretty deep pool of meanings: tiny, imperceptible, obscure, hidden, dim, subtle, what is obscured by darkness, etc. *Ming* has the opposite meaning: light, shine, vision, luminous, clearly discernible, etc. The phrase comes from an interplay of opposites: dark/light, or obscure/clear. One can translate *wei ming* as "subtle light" (Chan and Henricks), "faint enlightenment" (Lau), "subtle illumination" (Cleary), "hiding the light" (Pine), etc. The final two lines connect this obscure wisdom with the themes of verses 30 and 31.

37

Dao never acts upon anything,
yet nothing remains undone.
If rulers could hold to this,
all things would naturally transform themselves.
Thus transformed, if attachments should arise,
they are stilled with the pure simplicity of the Nameless.
This simplicity of the Nameless is empty of attachments.
Empty of attachments, there is tranquility,
and the world naturally settles into peace.

38

Highest virtue is not concerned with being virtuous and thus is true virtue.
Low virtue cannot let go of being virtuous and thus is false virtue.

A person of high virtue does not act on things, and is also free of intention.
A person of high benevolence does act, but without the intent of action.
A very righteous person acts with intent.
A rigidly ritualistic person acts, and if there's no response, rolls up his sleeves and forces it on people.

So, when the Way is lost, "being virtuous" arises.
This kind of virtue fails, so we resort to rules of benevolence.
This kind of benevolence fails, so we turn to righteousness.
When righteousness is lost, rules of ritualized conduct arise.
> Truly, rules and rituals are the thin dead husk of sincerity and
> good faith
> and the beginning of trouble and confusion.
> Ritual augury is concerned with the Dao's flower,
> but is the beginning of foolishness.

That is why the great person:
> stays with the substantial rather than the superficial,
> prefers the fruit to the flower,
> and rejects "that out there" to hold to "this in here."

39

Of ancient things that attained oneness:
>the heavens became one and thus clear,
>the Earth became one and thus firm,
>spirits became one and thus energized,
>empty valleys became one and thus filled with lushness,
>rulers became one and thus lead purely.

But, having reached oneness:
>if the heavens were ceaselessly clearing, they would rend;
>if the earth were always becoming firmer, it would crumble;
>if spirits were perpetually energetic, they would fizzle out;
>if valleys were always in growth, they would dry out;
>if rulers are honored and exalted without limit, they fall.

So then, honor has roots in humility, and the exalted need the foundation of lowliness. Hence, the custom of rulers calling themselves "the Orphaned One," "the Widowed One," and "the Unworthy One." Isn't this being rooted in humility?

Therefore they regard their many carriages the same as having no carriage.

Rather than tinkling and gleaming like jade they prefer to be solid as common rock.

Notes: There are two different ways of interpreting lines 7 through 12 (the second list of the results of attaining oneness). At issue is the intended meaning of the repeated phrase *wu yi* (without end, or unceasingly) in lines 2 through 6 and 8 through 12. In the standard texts, it is an instrumental *yi* meaning "If the sky were not *by it* clear..." etc. This instrumental *yi* gives the second section a different sense, something like:
"So, this implies that:
>if the Heavens were not made clear by it (by attaining oneness), they would rend;
>if the earth were not made firm by it, it would crumble;
>if spirits were not energized by it, they would fizzle out;
>if valleys were not in growth by it, they would reach end;
>if rulers were not made noble and exalted by it, they would fall."

This translation is basically just a reaffirmation of the first section, adding the consequences of what would happen if they didn't attain oneness: we then have *realizing* oneness (lines 2 through 6) vs. *lacking* oneness (lines 8 through 12). This is the interpretation adopted by a majority or translators: Bynner, Chan, Cleary, Feng and English, Hanson, Henricks, Hinton, Kwok, Palmer and Ramsay, Legge, Lin, Mabry, Mitchell, Star, Walker, Wu, and many others. It is the preferred sense of the later Fu Yi and standard texts.

In the Ma-wang-tui texts a final *yi* gives the sense "but if the sky were clear *without end (wu yi)...*" etc. My translation agrees with Lau and Pine who base theirs on the Ma-wang-tui texts (although Henricks uses the MWT and still prefers the other interpretation). My reasons for adopting the minority opinion are: 1) Both the Ho-shang Kung and Wang Pi commentaries support this interpretation, and 2) the second section is then more relevant than a simple reiteration of the first: keeping with an important theme of the *Dao De Jing*, even the positive characteristics of clarity, stability, energy, lushness of life, and leadership must avoid extremes and excess which would make them come to an end. Nature perpetuates only through the interplay of polarities. Indeed, the sky is not perpetually clear. Earth is not firm to the point of static immobility, or it would indeed crumble for want of shifting. A verdant valley must go through its seasonal cycles because perpetual growth cannot be sustained. All the polarities must keep each other from extremes, and *yin* and *yang* are in this way kept within the same circle, moving, transforming, and keeping the Earth and Heaven in motion.

40

The universal Way progresses by returning.
The universal Way accomplishes by yielding.
All below Heaven arise out of being,
but being arises from Emptiness!

41

A superior person hears of the Dao and diligently practices it.
An average person hears of the Dao and is sometimes aware, some-
times lost.
An inferior person hears of the Dao and laughs out loud.
If it isn't laughable, it isn't the Dao.
After all, it's the Dao which has given rise to these maxims:

> The luminous way appears dull,
> the way that leads forward seems to retreat,
> the smooth way seems rough,
> the highest virtue seems low and empty as a valley.
> great purity seems sullied,
> abundant virtue seems deficient,
> steadfast virtue seems flimsy,
> simple truth seems uncertain.
> It's like a great square that has no corners,
> A great tool that does nothing,
> A great melody that has no sound,
> A great image that has no shape!

The Way is always here, hidden in the background, nameless,
creating perfectly and completing perfectly.

42

Dao gives birth to the One,
the One gives birth to the two,
the Two gives birth to three,
and three gives birth to all the myriad things.
The myriad things carry *yin* at their backs and *yang* in their embrace;
being centered between these two energies produces harmony.

The world despises the orphaned, the desolate, and the unworthy,
and yet these are the names rulers use to refer to themselves.
Sometimes things gain by losing or lose by gaining.
What others have taught I also teach, namely this:
Those who live by force and aggression die by the same.
I see this as foundational.

Notes: "Tao gives birth to the beginning" says the Ho-Shang Kung commentary. It gives birth to the beginning of the universe by expressing itself as *yin* and *yang*, the energies of absorption and emission, respectively. Before the beginning, "the One" is the universal background which transcends the finiteness of separable things. "The two" are the fundamental forces of *yin* and *yang* (dark and bright, Earth and Heaven, female and male, absorption and emission). According to the Ho-shang Kung commentary, the *yin* breath and the *yang* breath give birth to the third, which is a "mixture of clear and murky." An organism (the third) is a mixture of the clear Heaven *qi* (life-force, breath) and the denser, turbid Earth *qi*.

All the myriad creatures "carry *yin* at their backs and *yang* in their embrace," and this is the blending of Heaven and Earth. Living in accord with the Dao means realizing you are centered between these two energies, and then harmonizing them. The final lines are examples of an approach to life which seeks the proper harmony between power and yielding, or gain and loss, rather than asserting one over the other.

43

What is most soft and yielding in the world
races easily over the hard things of the world.
What is without substance
penetrates where there are no spaces.
In this I understand the benefit of taking no action.
Few in the world can comprehend the
teaching that is without words,
and the success that is without effort.

44

Reputation or your body – which is dearer?
Your body or riches – which is worth more?
Gaining or losing – which is more distressing?
The more you desire, the more you spend;
the more you hoard, the greater your loss.
Know contentment right where you are and suffer no disgrace;
know when to stop so you suffer no harm and endure long.

45

The great Wholeness seems incomplete,
but using it you find it inexhaustible.
The great Fullness seems empty,
but using it you find it limitless.

Its great truth appears wrong,
its great skills appear crude,
its great surplus seems lacking,
and its great speech seems inarticulate.

Just as activity overcomes cold
and being still overcomes heat,
so also attaining clarity and stillness
makes you one with the ordering principle of the world.

46

When the world lives in accord with the Way,
the swiftest horses can go back to fertilizing fields.
When the world lives without the Way,
generations of warhorses are bred in the borderlands.
     There are no greater crimes than those born of greed.
     There is no greater calamity than not knowing contentment.
     There is no greater curse than habitual acquisition.
Knowing what is enough is the only abiding contentment!

47

Without stepping out the door,
you can know the whole cosmos.
Without looking out the window,
you can see Heaven's course.
The further one strays,
the less one knows.

So, the sage doesn't go elsewhere in order to know,
doesn't look elsewhere in order to understand,
and doesn't strive in order to accomplish.

48

Pursuing knowledge means accumulating daily;
pursuing the Dao means decreasing daily.
Decreasing oneself and decreasing again
Until one attains emptiness-action,
In which nothing is acting, yet nothing is left undone.

One who would govern must remain free of meddlesome busyness;
a busy-body is unqualified to govern.

49

A sage doesn't hold to a fixed mind.
Thus free, his mind becomes the mind of the people.

He treats good people with goodness;
and bad people he also treats with goodness.
In this way, goodness spreads.

He treats the faithful with faithfulness;
and the unfaithful he also treats with faithfulness.
In this way, faithfulness spreads.

You see, the sage is a unifying presence in the world,
his mind merging with others.
People's eyes and ears are wide open
but the sage's are covered.

Notes: In this verse we see the effect of the sage's inner state on the outer realm. Holding to the undivided gives the sage equanimity toward others. That "people's eyes and ears are wide open" means that they are distracted by the myriad appearances of the outside world (verse 1 spoke of the clinging mind perceiving a world of things, whereas the mind emptied of fixity and preconceptions perceives the hidden essence). That the sage's eyes and ears are covered means holding to the inward – a meditative abiding in Dao which affects the whole realm.

50

Life is an "emerging from" and death a "returning to."
The steps toward life are thirteen
and the steps toward death are thirteen.
People trying to add life to life still end up in the realm of death's
thirteen.
Why is this? Because they try too hard to live life.

But we hear of those skilled at sustaining life.
They walk the wilderness unconcerned about rhinos or tigers;
they enter battlefields without armor or weapons.
In them the rhino has no place to thrust its horn,
the tiger no place to use its claws,
the soldier no place to sink his sword.
How can this be?
They are empty of anything death can claim.

Note: The "thirteen" in lines 2 through 4 is *shi you san*, (literally "ten
have three") and is more commonly translated "three in ten" or "out
of ten, three..." or something similar (Bynner, Chan, Cleary, Hanson,
Lau, Legge, Mabry, Walker, and others). This popular interpretation
of *shi you san* also makes a very sensible translation:
Three out of ten (people) follow after life
and three out of ten follow after death.
Another three out of ten seek to augment life yet still end up with
death's thirteen.
Why? Because they live too forcefully.
Nevertheless, we hear of a person skilled at sustaining life.
Walking about, he doesn't avoid the rhinoceros or tiger...

Translating this way, nine out of ten people are accounted for in the
three groups of "three out of ten," and the tenth is the one who is
finally described variously as having no place for death to enter. Thus
"three out of ten" makes for a tidy interpretation. Nevertheless "thirteen" is preferred by Henricks, Lin, Pine, Wu, and a few others, who
see reference to the thirteen limbs and cavities through which life or
death enter, or the thirteen emotions and desires which enliven of

kill, or the thirteen days of the waxing and thirteen days of waning of the moon, all of which are significant in Daoist thinking. I was finally persuaded by Henricks, who noted that the unusual format, *shi-you* followed by a number, means ten plus that number in the I Ching, Mencius, and, significantly, in the Analects of Confucius 2:4, where we read "At the age of fifteen [*shi-you wu* meaning ten-plus-five] I set my heart on learning..." For a more complete discussion, see Henricks, p.123 and his note 57 on p. 269.

51

Dao gives birth to all things,
its power nourishes them,
matter gives them form,
and how they function completes their shape.
Thus are all things revering the Way and honoring its power.
Yet revering the Way and honoring its power are not for reward,
but arise naturally, spontaneously.

So, the Way brings things to life and nurtures them,
raises and completes them,
shelters them and gives them rest,
supports and protects them.
Creating without possessing,
acting without laying claim
raising without controlling–
this is called Deep Virtue.

Note: Deep Virtue is *xuan de*. *Xuan* means profound, secret, hidden, dark, or mysterious. *De* means virtue in the sense of power or effectiveness as well as goodness (see chapter 7 on the meaning of *de*). Wang Pi explains that there is a power present, a supreme effectiveness, but no one controls it or knows whence it comes; it comes from what is hidden or dark rather than from the bright and noisy world of the senses.

52

All below Heaven have a beginning
which may be called the Mother of the world.
When you come to know the Mother,
you can then recognize the children.
Having properly recognized the children,
you can return to abiding in the Mother,
and remain free of harm.

Close the mouth and shut the gates,
and throughout life you will avoid exhaustion.
As long as your mouth is going and you are busy about everything,
you remain beyond rescue.

To discern the small and subtle is illumination.
To remain gentle is strength.
When you follow light back to the source of illumination,
you don't get lost or suffer destruction.
You can call this "following the Eternal."

53

With a little natural understanding I can walk in the Great Way,
and my only fear would be to stray from it.
The great Way is smooth and easy to travel,
but people love to get side-tracked.
Just be aware of when things begin to get out of balance,
and you can remain centered in the Way.

Whenever the seats of government are very splendid,
you find the fields overrun with weeds and the granaries empty.
When officials are clothed in elegant finery and carrying sharpened swords,
and have too much food and drink and wealth beyond surplus;
this is robbery and arrogance, and certainly in opposition to the Way.

54

What is well planted is not uprooted;
what is well held does not slip away;
and will be honored from generation to generation without fail.
Cultivate it in your self,
and virtue will be genuine.
Cultivate it in your family,
and virtue will be plentiful.
Cultivate it in your village,
and virtue will endure.
Cultivate it in your nation,
and virtue will pervade.
Cultivate it in all beneath Heaven,
and virtue is spread throughout.

Evaluate virtue in each person from the standpoint of a person,
evaluate a family from the viewpoint of a family,
evaluate a village from the viewpoint of a village,
evaluate a nation from the viewpoint of a nation,
evaluate the world from the viewpoint of the world.
How do I understand that the world is like this? By this!

55

If one thoroughly embodies virtue
he is like a newborn infant
whom asps, scorpions, and vipers will not sting,
and birds of prey and wild beasts will not seize.
His bones are flexible and his muscles relaxed,
but his grip is firm!
He does not yet know the meeting of the sexes,
but his life-force is so vital that his organ becomes erect.
His harmony is so perfect that he can scream all day and not get hoarse.

To realize harmony is to be in accord with the eternal,
and being in accord with the eternal is called enlightenment.
But just seeking to lengthen your life is ill-fated.
Controlling your vital breath with the mind is forcing things.
Pushing anything to its prime only exhausts it,
and thus goes against the Way.
What goes against the Way soon comes to its end.

56

Those who know don't talk about it;
those who talk don't know.
> Close the mouth,
> shut the gates,
> soften the glare,
> join with the settling dust,
> blunt the sharp points,
> untangle the complications.

This is called the profound union.
In this union,
> there is no getting closer to or farther from,
> no gaining or losing
> no exalting or debasing.

And that's why nature honors it above all else.

57

Use straightforwardness to govern a state;
misdirection is for conducting battles.
Better yet, be empty of all such affairs and win the world!
How do I know this is indeed so?
By noticing this:

>the more restrictive the taboos, the poorer the people;
>the finer the weapons, the more troubled the State;
>the more ingenious the technology, the more bizarre things are made;
>the more issues become legal matters, the more people become criminals.

So, the sage says,

>I take no action, and the people transform themselves;
>I enjoy quietude, and the people correct themselves;
>I create no agendas, and the people prosper by themselves;
>I am free of attachments, and the people simplify their own lives.

Note: The way of the world is to add legislation to legislation, adjustment to adjustment, correction to correction, and complication to complication. Not trusting the world, one tries too hard to manage it, but the way of the Dao is to be empty of artifice and manipulations. The leader who abides in spiritual connection to the Dao affects the whole realm by his connection, as described in the last four lines.

58

    When the government is dulled and unobtrusive
    people live simply and wholesomely.
    Where the government is sharp and prying
    people become restless and contentious.
    Bad fortune rides on good fortune,
    and good fortune is concealed in bad fortune
So, who knows which is the ultimate outcome?
There is no ordered norm.
What is "as it should be" turns into what "ought not to be,"
and what is meant for good becomes something sinister.
People have been confused for a long time.
    Therefore, the sage is a straight edge, but doesn't cut;
    is sharp, but doesn't stab;
    is straightforward, but not severe;
    is illuminating, but not blinding.

59

In governing people and attending to Heaven
there's nothing better than moderation.
In moderation one is yielding from the start.
"Yielding from the start" means abundant cultivation of virtue.
Abundant cultivation of virtue means anything can be overcome.
That anything can be overcome means knowing no limitations.
Knowing no limitations makes one fit to guard the country.
It is by guarding the country's Mother that one endures long.
This is called having deep roots and a sturdy trunk –
the way to long life and enduring vision.

60

Rule a great state as gently as you would cook a small fish.
If you govern a nation in accord with the Way
spiritual beings will have no power.
It's not that they lose their power;
it's that their power does not harm anyone.
It's not just that their power does not harm anyone;
but the sage himself also harms no one.
Since neither harms others,
virtue is combined and returns to both.

61

A great state is like a lowland river basin.
It is the female aspect of the world –
a place of confluence for the world,
In passive repose the female overcomes the male.
For this stillness she assumes the position underneath.

A great state may take the lower position for a small state
and thus absorb the small state.
A small state may lower itself for a great state
and thus win over the great state.
Thus, some benefit by lowering themselves,
and others benefit by being lower.
A great state wants to unify and feed its people;
a small state wants to have its service welcomed.
So truly, for both to obtain what they want,
the greater should act as the lower.

62

Dao is the place of confluence for all things: they flow toward it
naturally.
It is the good person's treasure-house,
and the bad person's refuge.
Beautiful words get used like currency,
and noble actions get presented as a gift.
But even if a person is no good at these,
why should he be rejected?

When crowning an emperor or installing ministers of state,
rather than presenting jade and teams of horses,
it would be better to kneel and present this Dao.

This is why the ancients honor it so.
Didn't they say that those who seek find,
and those who commit offenses are forgiven?
This is why Dao is the whole world's treasure.

63

Act without acting;
go about your business without busyness;
savor what is without flavor.
Great or small, many or few,
repay wrongs with kindness.
Plan for difficulties while they're still easy,
and deal with great matters while they're small.
Truly, the world's difficult affairs start out easy
and its great affairs start out small.
Therefore the sage never has to act in a big way to accomplish
great things.
Agreeing too easily makes one untrustworthy,
and taking it too easy lets difficulties arise.
So, the sage is wary of difficulties
and thus avoids them altogether.

64

What is still peaceful is easily held.
What is not yet manifest is easily planned for.
What is still thin is easily broken.
What is still small is easily scattered.
Deal with things before they come into fruition.
Set things in order before there is disorder.

A tree too wide to wrap your arms around grows from a tiny seed.
A nine-story tower begins with a single bucket of clay.
A journey of hundreds of miles begins with lifting a foot.

He who acts ruins.
He who clings loses hold.
Therefore, the sage does not act and thus does not ruin,
does not cling and thus does not lose anything.
People pursuing enterprises always fail in this just before completion.
That's why it is said:
Careful to the end as you are at the beginning,
and your enterprise will not fail.

So, the sage only desires freedom from desires,
and does not covet things just because they are hard to obtain.
Learning the art of unlearning, he returns to what the people missed.
But to help the world return to what is *of itself* so–
he cannot presume to act upon it.

65

It's said that the ancient ones, skilled in the practice of the Way,
did not enlighten the people with knowledge,
but made sure they could remain simple.
What makes the people unruly is knowledge.
    Thus, ruling by knowledge brings ruin to a country;
    Ruling by not-knowing brings Virtue to a country.
Who understands these two principles knows the normative model.
This is called deep virtue!
Deep virtue reaches deep and reaches far
to gather all things to return,
and therein they realize the Great Harmony.

Note: For the problem with knowledge discussed here, see the note on verse 3. In this verse, the "knowledge" that makes the people unruly or hard to govern is described in the Ho-shang Kung commentary as "cunning know-how and conventional wisdom" with its emphasis on propriety, societal convention, and other traditional values that come from thinking that is out of touch with nature and simplicity. So, people use knowledge to become clever and deceitful. "Ruling by knowledge" likely has to do with political cunning which is calculating rather than straightforward, and seeks to manipulate the people rather than let them be natural. Ho-shang Kung says such leaders "will always forsake the Way and virtue, abuse their power, and become the enemy of the country." In contrast, when political affairs are not managed by politically clever people, "then the people will remain fair and honest, and will not become perverse and hypocritical....This is the good fortune of the country." Alan K.L. Chan, *Two Visions of the Way*, pp. 153, 154.

66

How does the ocean govern the flowing of a hundred river valleys?
Its skill lies in simply being the lowest.
That's how it is able to govern a hundred river valleys.

In the same way, a sage who would oversee the people
must speak as one below them;
desiring to lead the people,
must put himself behind them.

In this way, the sage can be above without being a burden,
and can lead without getting in the way.
People can support this kind of leader joyfully and without tiring.
A wise person does not contend with the world,
and with such a one no one can contend.

67

The world calls me great –
    great, but a misfit.
Really, it's only because I don't fit in that I am able to be great.
If I fit in, I would be trivial.
    But I always have three treasures that I guard and cherish:
    The first is compassion,
    the second is frugality,
    the third is reluctance to put myself first in the world.
    Compassion allows there to be courage;
    frugality allows there to be generosity;
    reluctance to put oneself first allows development of full leadership.

Now, if you try to be courageous without compassion,
or try to be generous, but forsake frugality,
or try to lead , but forsake the reluctance to be first,
doom follows inevitably.

However, with compassion,
you remain victorious when attacked
and when defending you are invincible.
What Heaven establishes it protects through compassion.

68

The most skillful military officer is never warlike;
the most skillful fighter is never angry;
the most skillful victor does not engage confrontation;
the most skillful manager places himself below others.
This is called the virtue of non-aggression.
It is called utilizing the other's energy and blending it with heaven.
There is no higher principle!

69

Military strategists say:
> Rather than daring to initiate, it's better to respond.
> Rather than pushing forward an inch, it's better to retreat a foot.

This is what's known as:
> advancing without a forward march,
> seizing without arms,
> capturing without attacking,
> holding without weapons.

There's no greater misfortune than underestimating an enemy,
and risking the loss of my treasures.
When armies face off, all things being equal,
the side rueful about battle will win.

70

My words are very easy to understand,
and very easy to practice.
Yet in the world few understand;
few put them into practice.

My words have an Ancestor;
my deeds have a Lord.
It's because people don't understand Them
that they don't understand me.

When those who understand me are few,
then I am highly valued.
Behold the sage:
    Outwardly, dressed in a peasant's coarse cloth;
    inwardly, carrying priceless jade.

71

Knowing you don't know is best;
not knowing you don't know brings affliction.
The sage is without affliction because,
recognizing afflictions for what they are,
she stays free from them.

72

If the people lose their fear of authorities,
a greater dread befalls them.
So, do not constrict the size of their dwelling places;
do not oppress their means of living.
Truly, don't oppress them if you don't want them agitated.

The sage knows who he is and has no need to make a show of himself;
loves himself, but does not make a treasure of himself;
has let go of "that out there," and holds to "this in here."

73

The courage to take bold actions often gets one killed;
the courage to not take bold actions preserves life.
But for either of these, there is sometimes benefit, sometimes harm.
Who knows why heaven rejects what it does?
Heaven's Way
     does not fight, yet is excellent at winning;
     does not speak, yet has perfect response;
     is not summoned, yet appears on its own;
     is never hurried nor worried, yet plans excellently.
Heaven's net is vast, and though wide-meshed, nothing slips past it.

74

If people do not fear death, why threaten them with capital punishment?
If they are under constant dread of death, yet still act unlawfully,
then those we catch and arrest we'd have to kill,
and who would dare do that?
There is already a Grim Reaper, and taking his place is like
stepping in to wield the blade of a master wood-carver.
Whoever does this rarely escapes injuring himself.

Note: This rather unusual verse is about the futility and dangers of
excessive punishment. The more oppressive and punitive the ruler,
the less people fear death because life becomes anxious and burdensome. The more capital punishment is used, the more people
become lawless. This verse exhorts rulers to resort first to the Dao
for correcting the people (compare verse 57) in order to avoid correcting by ever more excessive punishments.

"Grim Reaper" seems a reasonably close concept in English for
si ze, meaning Great Executioner, or Lord of Death. Lu Hui-ch'ing
(1031-1111) and Su Ch'e (1039-1112) comment that the executioner is heaven, and we should not take it on ourselves to kill those
whom heaven may not have abandoned. Wing-tsit Chan also sees *si
ze* as referring to heaven and translates it thus in his excellent book,
The Way of Lao Tzu. This makes good sense of the last line, that
capital punishment is like presuming to do what should only be in
Heaven's timing.

75

The reason people are starving
is because their rulers eat up too much tax-grain.
That's why they starve.
The reason the people are difficult to govern
is because their rulers always find reasons for meddlesome actions.
That's why they become difficult to govern.
The reason the people are unconcerned about death
is because having to strive for life has made it burdensome.
That's why they're unconcerned about death.

Truly, one who does not strive for life is even wiser than one who reveres life.

76

When life begins we are supple and tender.
When life ends we are rigid and unyielding.
All things, including the grass and trees,
are pliant and supple in life,
and dry and rigid in death.
So the supple and tender are companions of life,
While the stiff and unyielding are companions of death.

> An army that cannot yield is defeated.
> A tree that can't bend cracks in the wind.
> The strong and great are laid low
> while the soft and gentle prevail.

77

The Way of Heaven is like the drawing of a bow:
>The higher part is drawn downward,
>and the lower part draws upward.
>Where there is excess it diminishes;
>and where there is lack, it supplies.

Heaven's Way takes from what is excessive, and supplements what isn't enough.
Humanity's way is not like this, is it?
We take from those not having enough and make offerings to the rich.
Who can find the abundance and give it to the world? Only a person of the Way.
And so the sage:
>acts without claiming merit,
>accomplishes without dwelling on it.

In being like this, there is no desire to be seen as virtuous.

78

Below Heaven there is nothing so soft and yielding as water.
And yet for attacking the strong and unyielding, nothing surpasses it.
For this reason, nothing can take its place.
> The yielding overcomes the unyielding,
> and the soft overcomes the hard.
Everyone recognizes this, but few practice it.
Therefore the sage says:
> Who takes the country's dishonors on oneself
> is worthy of the sacred offerings for soil and grain;
> Who takes a country's misfortunes on oneself
> is worthy of being king.
(Straight truth often sounds twisted.)

79

Even in resolving great disputes
the residue of dispute remains.
So, how can this be "making good?"
Therefore, the sage assumes the debtor's portion and makes no demands on others.
Those who possess virtue attend to their obligations;
while those with no virtue attend to the exaction of payment.
Heaven's Way is without partiality,
but always abides with the good person.

Notes: In the days the *Dao De Jing* was written, loan agreements and figures were written on a bamboo stick and then the stick was split lengthwise, creating two interlocking pieces. The left side was the "inferior" side which belonged to the debtor. The right was the "superior" side held by the creditor. In paying off the loan, the debtor (holder of the left side) is giving, but only what is due; he is obviously not expecting merit or praise in return. The Way of Virtue transcends this convention with something higher, because "even in resolving great disputes, the residue of dispute remains, and how can this be making good?" So, the sage is one who in life "assumes the debtor's portion" and makes no demands on others."

80

Societies should be no larger than villages.
Then there is no need for an abundance of inventions.
People who understand mortality stop running to and fro;
even with an abundance of transports, there is no need for them.
And if they have armaments, there is no occasion to display them.
Let life be simple enough for:

remembering things by knotting a string,
making good meals and beautiful clothing,
enjoying the peacefulness of home,
and finding joy in the everyday.

Villages close enough to hear each other's dogs and roosters,
could live their entire lives without feeling compelled to travel back
and forth.

81

Trustworthy words are not elegant;
elegant words are not trustworthy.
Those who understand are not widely learned;
the widely learned do not necessarily understand.
Those who are good avoid debate;
skill at debate does not mean you are good.

The sage does not accumulate.
The more he acts for others the more he himself has.
In giving everything away he finds abundant richness.
Heaven's Way is to bring benefit, but at no one's expense.
The sage's actions always accord with Heaven's.

Chang dao (eternal dao)

Dao: the Way of Returning

Traditionally, the hermitage of the Daoist sage was small and almost empty of "stuff." The Daoist reveals little interest in accumulating things, but this is not some sort of ascetic self-denial. Rather, the sage is one who is no longer entranced by perpetual gain, has no desire for shiny, noisy things, and has no ambitions for a life of business, busyness, accumulation, or status-seeking. What does one do in these circumstances? The sage leaves for a place well beyond the never-settling dust of the marketplace and the anxious noise of commerce, a place unreachable by the arrogant rattling of an official's carriage. The sage's home is nature – and nature, in Chinese thought, is the realm of "that which happens of itself," which is the meaning of the Chinese characters for Nature (*ziran*). So, liberated from delusions of the unnatural realm (perpetual gain, status, control, etc.,) the sage seeks a remote place of naturalness and calm, free from distractions, and conducive to a meditative life, enjoying each day to its fullest, or even wandering for a few days without any specific purpose or goal.

Who is this sage? A person in tune, or *inwardly attuned to*, the natural world and the Universe itself. More accurately, the sage is one is attuned to the subtle "essence" (*miao*) that is silently and invisibly behind this universe of "things." That there is such a hidden essence is attested by Laozi in such enigmatic statements as "How do I know this is so? By things as they are" or "By this in here," referring to a state of presence, completely beyond the grasping of thoughts, but which is in tune with the universal wholeness. This sounds mystical, because, well, it is. But many of today's most renowned scientists affirm a universal wholeness. David Bohm and B.J. Hiley, two modern deep-thinking physicists, reject the old atomistic view that the universe is built, fundamentally, of infinitesimal parts: "Rather, we say that inseparable quantum interconnectedness of the whole universe is the fundamental reality, and that relatively independent behaving parts are merely particular and contingent forms within this whole."[2]

Inseparable interconnectedness as the fundamental reality. The new physics, if we care to be scientific, sees the universe as a *holistic* system, that is, more like *organism* than mechanism. Whether atoms, or bio-systems in nature, or the intricate balances necessary for entire galaxies to exist, the more complete and fundamental picture is one if integral wholeness.

At least twenty-five centuries ago, the "sage" or "superior person" was an adept who perceived this absolutely fundamental, if subtle, wholeness. In Daoist sensibilities, the perfect person is one who most perfectly integrates heaven and earth as one. He or she is quite at home in nature and does not strive against its unrefined spontaneity.

On cold mountains or in emerald valleys, amid the cries of gibbons and hawks, the wise one's only ambition is to embrace the Universal Way without straying. Do you have to do it among gibbons and hawks? No, it's just easier. But you can also do it among the modern day gibbons in suits and ties in the noisiest purpose-driven market-place. Preferably, we each find our own balance and the place in which we can best remain attuned.

Centuries ago, the everyday activities of the Daoist sage might consist of hoeing a potato bed, gathering dry leaves for the tea stove, gathering windfall firewood, and letting a sun-warmed boulder

---

2 David J. Bohm and B.J. Hiley, "On the Intuitive Understanding of Nonlocality as Implied by Quantum Theory", *Foundations of Physics* Vol 5 (1975)

serve as bed, the sky as roof for an afternoon nap. Returning to the uncontrived life, one realizes the eternal Dao flows through one's entire being just as it flows through everything else. An uncluttered hut is sufficient for a dinner of vegetables, some stored rice, perhaps some chrysanthemum wine enjoyed with a cliff-dwelling neighbor. Laughter lingers over the drying ink of wine-inspired poems, until they are both surprised by the returning sun. Compared to this, the god of commerce and business is a bland pretender.

Zhuangzi (Chuang-tzu, Section 13, "The Way of Heaven), of the late fourth century BCE, explains that the sage's retreat from delusion-driven ambitions is not a willful act toward some spiritual end. Rather, it is the natural outcome of his or her spiritual state:

> The non-action of the wise man is not simply inaction.
> It is not a studied thing and thus cannot be upset by anything.
> The sage is quiet, not because he *wills* to be quiet
> but because he is not unsettled.
> Still water is like glass:
> looking in it you can see even the bristles on your chin.
> Also it is so perfect a level that a carpenter can use it.
> If water can be so clear and so level,
> how much more the spirit?
> The heart of the wise man is this tranquil
> and as such, is the mirror of heaven and earth,
> the glass of *everything*.
> Emptiness, stillness, tranquility, tastelessness, silence,
> non-action:
> these describe the level of heaven and earth.
> This is perfect Dao and here sages find their resting place.
> Resting, they are empty of delusions.

A person of the Way (*Dao*) recognizes a Universe in which *we are integral aspects of the whole*. As such, one cultivates a life of integration, balance, and flow, and assumes a peculiar kind of ease to living. This is because when one flows *with* the universal Way one will naturally perceive the entire Universe going alongside, just as the current of a great river seems to "go along with" anyone who swims *with* it rather than against it. We may contrast this with the mental attitude of asserting ourselves as separate entities who "know better" what is good for us. A man swimming hard against the current of a great river expends much energy for a progress only apparent to the very limited perspective of the swimmer.

The person of Dao tends to be more at ease with existence because of a recognition that so-called opposites are secretly in harmony with each other. With this understanding, one no longer strives to make one side win, nor does one live in anxiety about its opposite side. The wise person has discovered that the interplay of "opposing" forces is *necessary to the functioning of the universe.* Wanting all growth or light with no decay or dark is simply an absurdity of human thinking. The Dao is always in harmony, and, living attuned to it, one never performs any action amiss.

Anyone entranced by thoughts of ever-increasing power or accumulation will find this Way of returning to what is natural laughable or even subversive. Laozi knows this, and affirms:

> "A superior person hears of the Way and diligently practices it.
> An average person hears of the Way and is sometimes aware, sometimes lost.
> An inferior person hears of the Way and laughs aloud.
> If he didn't laugh it couldn't be the Way" (verse 41).

Why laugh about the path known as Dao? Because it utterly contradicts so many of our long-held assumptions. Its luminescence appears dull to us, and its truths are often paradoxical. The Way finds progress in retreating, is happy with what is low and rough rather than high and refined, knows the purity of what seems sullied, finds greater value in *less* rather than more, and sees the greatest power and resilience in what is gentle and yielding. Further, the Dao is said to be "like a great tool that does nothing, a melody that is silent, a great pattern that is formless." Laughable, inscrutable, or profound, it invites us to follow a universal way which contradicts our conventional illusions.

The word *Dao* commonly means a way, a path or road. The path that Laozi teaches leads is, in a sense, backwards to our way of thinking. This is because it is a way of return to who we really were before we learned to be unnatural, to the world as it really *is* before we learned to see it as an object with which we struggle. The author and translator Red Pine follows the scholar of comparative religions, John Tu Er-wei (1913-1987), in seeing in the Chinese character *dao* a likely reference to the path of the moon as it moves through its phases of light and dark.[3]

Like the moon, everything in nature cycles through phases of expansion and contraction, bright and dark, going forth and returning, birth and death. The world pursues only growth, expansion, and fullness to their limits, but nature is cyclic, and the only place to go from gain and expansion is into the phase of loss or contraction, just like a waning moon. The wise person rides the small that is about to grow, the dim that is about to become brighter, and thus prefers the beginning rather than the end of each cycle. This is a repeated theme throughout the *Dao De Jing*.

Though there is a religious branch of Daoism, the Dao is not really an object of religion; it is not another word for God; it is not even some thing to be "believed in" via any sort of doctrine. It requires no divinely revealed knowledge, issues no commandments, compels no actions, and employs no hierarchies because it exercises no authority. Indeed, it sees the Universe as running not by any authority but by its own dynamic *interrelations*. A reasonable person does not, when planting a seed, command it to grow, because *it is already the seed's nature* to do so.

The natural world does not run by authority, but by the spontaneity of *life*: nature is what happens of itself. The Chinese word for nature reflects this principle: "nature" is *ziran*, or "of itself so." Plants grow spontaneously *because it is their nature to do so*, not because of any authority compelling them. Also, the nature of the plant is intricately interwoven to the manifold nature of its environment, inextricably. The environment produces the plants, and the plants make up the environment.

---

3   See Red Pine, *Lao-tzu's Taoteching* (San Francisco: Mercury House, 2001) the introduction.

But we humans have come to think of ourselves as different from– even *separate* from– Nature. This is perhaps our most destructive delusion. We forget that the planet produced us in the same manner as it did the plants and other animals. At one time our planet was dead rock surrounded in poisonous gasses, rife with volcanic activity, and utterly inhospitable to life. Nevertheless! Here we all are. And we exist together by subtle balances in a state of complete interrelatedness.

Interfere with one part, and that interference ripples throughout the whole. We are organisms and our earth is the environment, and environments always produce and shape their organisms. As obvious as this should be, the philosopher Alan Watts had to remind western audiences that, "just as an apple tree produces apples," so the earth produces people; we are not foreigners to this life-producing planet. He also reminded audiences, "you did not come *into* this world; you came *out of* it!" When you mistakenly feel alien from our planet, you are capable of all sorts of destructive behavior, asserting "improvements" in ignorance of the delicately balanced intricacies nature produces.

It is helpful to always remember that we *emerged from* the ordering principle inherent in the planet, and the planet emerged from an ordering principle inherent in the galaxy, and you can follow this outward until you discover the universe itself producing what you have come to think of as you! Is there an intelligent Designer behind the universe's inherent intelligence? If you need to look at it that way, that is fine, but the author(s) of the *Dao De Jing* did not conceive of an outside-the-box divinity necessary for creating this self-regulating natural order. In verse four, Laozi says of the Dao "I do not know from whom it could have come; it seems to have preceded even *Di*" (the lord of creation in old Chinese mythology).

This creative and ordering principle is felt to be *inherent within* the Universe itself, and simply does not require an external cause. Theists may chafe against this point, but the *Dao* is not a wholly-other cosmic monarch making things happen by divine authority. Here, reliance on external powers and authorities is but a symptom of troublesome thinking and its unnatural practices. Instead, the Dao's power (virtue) is to create without possessing or laying claim, to nurture without controlling. Though the Dao does not "act upon" anything, nothing in the natural world is left undone.

The wisdom of the Laozi book is such that it tells of nowhere else one must go, and nothing unnatural for which one must reach. *Dao* is what is already here because it is the hidden essence of existence itself. Similar to "the Force" in Star Wars, this universal hidden essence is everywhere and in everything. It is what is here all the time. We walk in it whether or not we recognize it. When we feel apart from it we strive with life; when we recognize it we flow with life.

So, what is this Dao?

The first verse of the *Dao De Jing* is not so much a philosophical statement as an expression of an enlightened state in which one experiences first-hand, or *directly*, the essential unity of all things. Behind all the apparent forms in this world, which appear as separable and differentiated, an enlightened psyche perceives the subtle Oneness underlying all the varied manifestations. That which does the manifesting is prior to its manifested world of "things." It is beyond forms, concepts, words, and even space or time.

Well then, is the Dao perceivable? Not as a thing. Laozi says, "Looking for it, we see nothing and call it invisible. Listening, we hear nothing and call it inaudible. Grasping, there is nothing to get hold of and we call it intangible."

So, how is Dao perceived? According to verse 1, we sense it in a state of mind described as *wu yü*, which means not just "without desires" but emptied of preconceptions, that is, a meditative mind which has gone deeper than its habitual thought constructs or mental patterns. Dao is perceived in stillness, or a *quiet centeredness*, with "eyes and ears closed off" from the world of sensory stimulation. And after it is perceived, one is unable to adequately describe the experience, and must resort to metaphor: "With Dao, [in that state of enlightenment], sharp edges are rounded off, complications are unraveled, harsh light is softened, even dust settles into place. So still and clear, it seems barely present..."

In this enlightened state, the experience of the universe as a unity penetrates deeply. Our so-called opposites are found to be mutually-arising polarities of the One. The hidden essence under-lying or in all things is felt to be *the fundamental* reality, an unfrag-mented reality. All manifestations, that is, "the ten-thousand things," are felt to be a conditional reality – the merely empirical. Perception of the world as separate objects is introduced through the condi-tioned mind with its desires and deep-seated mental patterns. We reinforce differentiation by naming "parts" of what is essentially, but subtly, a unity.

In this deeper view, all objects are objects of consciousness. That our everyday world of "ten-thousand things" is secretly a unity with this unfragmented hidden essence is *the* "primal mystery." Can one know this primal mystery? Verse 1 proposes that it is indeed possi-ble to perceive "the Origin hidden beneath all origins, the gateway to everything's mysterious essence."

As a verb, *Dao* can also mean speak, or be spoken of. The *Dao De Jing* tells us at the outset: "A way (*Dao*) that can be spoken (*Dao*) is not the eternal (or constant, immutable) Way (*Dao*)." There are numerous possible translations, such as, "The way that can be spoken of is not the unchanging Way," or "The path that can be fol-lowed is not the eternal Dao itself."

No matter which way one chooses to translate the Chinese text, the point is basically the same: what we can talk about or practice is relative and changing and therefore only *points toward* the absolute, eternal, or constant Way which remains invisible, silent, intangible, and beyond our words. Zhuangzi (25:11) said:

> To name it "Dao" is to name what is not a thing.
>
> It cannot be named like created or conditional things.
> Concepts such as "caused" or "by chance" have no bearing on the Dao.
> Calling it "Dao" only indicates without defining.
>
> Dao is beyond words; it is beyond objects.
> It can be expressed neither by words nor by silence.
> In the frame of mind hanging between words and silence Dao is understood.

Though Dao is not to be confused with the Western concept of God, the statement, "The *dao* we can talk about is not the unchanging *Dao*" is analogous to saying, in western religious terms, "Let us not confuse our concepts of God with God," or, "As soon as we talk about God, it's no longer God we are talking about." Nevertheless, when a theist, whether Jewish, Christian, or Muslim, reads Laozi for the first time, the question naturally arises, "Is the Dao the same as God?" This is because it is spoken of in absolute terms and as the source and end of all creation. But the Tao is not a personality, not willful, and not an authority figure. I do like the Rev. John R. Mabry's suggestion that "the Tao is God *as nature sees* God." Every other creature is also a part of nature, of "creation," but they lack hierarchical concepts and divisions such as: divine versus natural, holy versus mundane, lofty versus lowly, heavenly versus earthly, and any concept of a grand Person running everything. Nevertheless, they interact with the Dao, and are essential aspects of it. Nature sees "God" in Daoist simplicity.

Beyond words and concepts

In its highest form, Laozi's wisdom must be conveyed in a "teaching without words." The eternal is wordless. The Sufi mystic Rumi said, "Silence is the language of God, all else is poor translation." Later, Fr. Thomas Keating elaborated, "Silence is God's first language; everything else is a poor translation. In order to hear that language, we must learn to be still and to rest in God." Reality is always greater than what we can describe of it, even in finite matters. Words are already not the truth, because they are but symbols pointing to a reality, which is why one cannot quench thirst with the word "water."

The *Dao De Jing*, in designating the aspect of Dao that is beyond our words, uses *chang dao*, which basically means the constant, or immutable, or timeless Dao. Some have translated it as the "everlasting way," "the Absolute," or "the Eternal Way." Others caution that the Chinese of old probably did not share exactly our concepts of transcendence or eternity. The nearest approximation to a transcendent reality or the eternal would be that above all, (and *underlying* all), is the *Dao* and its outworking power (*de*) from which all life springs and to which all things return. Transcendence should also be thought of as *beneath* all – that which is *underlying* and *supporting* all phenomena. Though elusive to concepts or words, it is as inescapable and constant as the "now" moment in which we actually live but of which we have little awareness. In Asian thought, the everlasting, absolute, or eternal is not so very far away. You are *in* it, (and, in the same way that an apple is the tree, you *are* the Dao) whether you recognize it or not!

The Dao of now: a path to the present

Past and future are purely mental, that is, memories or anticipations. But because the mind wants to live almost exclusively in the past or future, we get confused and feel they are real, maybe even more real than the present. After all, how small is *now*? How short it is! –when we conceptualize time in a linear fashion. It seems to be infinitely divisible into an ever smaller slice between lost past and future (both of which seem to go on forever, if only in our heads). So it is the habit of our minds to dwell with past or future rather than with what is actually before us. And this creates the discontentment of feeling disconnected from life itself, because life is always happening *now*. Life always occurs as *this moment, right here, and right now.* That is the last thing we think about! Missing it, we grasp for more and more of life, or for a longer life so we can get it later, and find ourselves wishing we had "more time." But there is no such thing as more time; we never actually have *time*; we have *now*. A person always needing "more time" probably just needs fewer activities.

A sage of old said, "Intimate with Dao each morning, one could die in contentment any evening." If we want to know contentment and peace, the old sage points us toward the *chang Dao*, the everlasting or constant Way. And what is more everlasting than now? Isn't it *always* now? And yet *now* is never fully penetrated by the intellect, and cannot be fully described; now cannot be grasped because you never actually leave it, except in your mind.

Because Dao is now, and because it is beyond words, it is, paradoxically, beyond seeking. How can I seek for *here*? How can I wait for *now*? Dao is already right here, and discovering it feels like returning home to something we have always known in the recesses of our minds, that is, to what is most natural, uncontrived, and uncomplicated. Confucius is reported to have explained: "Dao is that from which you cannot depart; if you can depart from it, it isn't the Dao."[4] No group or religion has exclusive access to the Dao. It operates for all alike, nurturing all things, and making no demands.

Though the eternal Dao is right here, and right now, it is hidden to the busy mind, the goal-oriented and grasping mind, the future-based mind. The *eternal*, with which we long for connection, is always happening *now*. And *right here*. It is the mind that has strayed elsewhere. This is an odd thought to anyone who has grown up with the unexamined assumption that eternity is something that happens before we were born (eternal past) and after we die (either an eternal future in which we no longer exist, or an eternal afterlife in which we do).

Attaching significance only to past or future, we miss the tune of eternity which is always heard *now*. Admittedly, this discussion of time and eternity is not an explicit theme of the *Dao De Jing*, but it is important to understand how what might be called "eternal" in an Asian context differs from ideas of eternity prevalent among modern westerners.

In great spiritual traditions, Hindu, Buddhist, Jewish, Christian, and others, the breakthrough of spiritual insight results in an inversion of our notion of time. To the rare person who wakes up to the reality of the present, the past and future are seen as nothing but memories or anticipations, that is, as mental imagery. The future is nothing but the mind's dream until an event becomes *present*. Likewise, the past is memory which is remembered *now*.

So, one never really leaves the present. But that's okay, because the present *is* eternity. The key is to realize that the present is all that ever has existed, like a seamless, eternal now-moment, transcending the time-world of clocks, calendars and day planners. Eternity transcends time, but is mentally shut off by our psychological experience

---

4   From the *Chungyung*, attributed to the grandson of Confucius.

of time, so we miss it.[5] In the West we have confused eternity with "forever," which is a duration of *time*. One never finds eternity in time; eternity remains hidden from our psychological time-world. It is here and now, constantly. Likewise, the transcendent is hidden in the here-and-now, and not in some future time nor other place.

This long digression is to make a point. The eternal Tao is not to be confused with contemporary Western notions of a transcendent time and space outside of the natural world. In the East, what is to be transcended is our limited understanding of *this* world! So, in the *Dao De Jing* we are brought back again and again to basing our lives on what is "constant." And this has to do not only with penetrating what is here and now, but also with understanding the "real" to be that which is unconditioned, or happening of itself.

Existence flows.

An attitude of anxious rigidity comes from uselessly clinging to things that are by nature in flux. This grasping after fixity is a futility that only leads to exhaustion and, often, suffering. The philosopher Alan Watts said, "It must be obvious...that there is a contradiction in wanting to be perfectly secure in a Universe whose very nature

---

5   Risking the readers patience, we can pursue this a bit further and see that our Western notion of eternity as a duration of time in a heavenly realm is counter to its own religious roots. It is curious that cultures with Judeo-Christian heritage have come to confuse eternity with "forever," when their earliest spiritual traditions actually find eternity in the present. The Hebrew name for God means "I Am that I Am," or, we could say, the One Who is Eternally *Present*. According to the Gospel attributed to John, Jesus said, somewhat esoterically, "Before Abraham was, I *am*." The change in verb tense is instructive: it reflects the recognition that what is ultimately real transcends time and can only be expressed in terms of the present. Also in that same Gospel, Jesus understands "eternal life" as a *present* union: "This is eternal life, that a person may know the Father..." In the Gospel of Thomas the disciples ask Jesus to tell them who he is so that they may believe in him. He tells them, "You search all over Heaven and earth, but do not know what is in front of your faces, nor do you know how to discern this present moment" (saying 91). When the disciples ask Jesus when the kingdom would come, he tells them that the kingdom is already spread out all over the earth and people simply do not recognize it (saying 113).

is momentariness and fluidity."[6] When we talk about the Way being "constant," or "everlasting" or "eternal" we do not mean permanently the same or rigidly fixed in form. The Dao has no form. Just like the present moment, it is in perpetual transformation. The Greek philosopher Heraclitus observed, "Everything flows," and "You don't step into the same river twice." The natural world reveals continual flow and change, but underlying all its myriad and changing manifestations is *something* formless, a subtle oneness. This is the *Way* that is constant, or "eternal," the *chang dao*.

Similarly, the outworking power of Dao, usually called its "virtue," is *chang de*, or the unfaltering virtue. It is precisely because it remains in a continually self-balancing ebb and flow that it lasts and is inexhaustible. Metaphorically, the Dao is not something you stand on rigidly and firmly, fists on hips; it is the universal current in which you swim. Though it gives rise to all forms, it has no form of its own. Some translators avoid rendering *chang* as "eternal" because they feel the term confuses readers with Western notions of transcendence, but I feel, for the reasons given above, that "eternal" aptly describes the hidden constant underlying this ever changing world, and personally, the word "eternal" resonates for me. You may prefer another term which resonates with you.

It is this transcendent aspect of the Dao that encompasses both physical existence and non-existence, and is beyond our intellectual grasp so that words never quite reach it. Our names and concepts and philosophical categories have no bearing on the Dao. Those who know cannot find the words; those who rely on words do not know. That being said, there is an aspect of Dao that we talk (and write) about, and that is why there is a *Dao De Jing*, with a little over five thousand words comprising eighty-one short verses.

In its *out*working power, Dao is found in the observable, describable way of the Universe— what we see in nature. We observe nature's norms and rhythms, the polarities underlying everything, the inherent intelligence of nature, and self-balancing flow of forces making up the Universe and all that is in it, including ourselves. Inasmuch as we are an aspect of the greater whole, flow is also the

---

6   Alan Watts, in *The Wisdom of Insecurity* (1951)

proper and natural state for our own lives. A rigid approach to life interrupts flow because it demands divisive thinking, hierarchical conceptions, and the attempt to force things unnaturally. The martial art and exercises of Taiji (Tai Chi) are rooted in Dao and thus it is an utterly non-rigid art, beautiful to watch, healthful to perform, and deceptively effective as a martial art. Practicing any Daoist art means seeking only to move or act with the subtle universal current. Thus it implies that the greatest success will be found in ease and naturalness. As we learn to flow *with* it, the power of the Dao is underlying and in our actions.

In relation to this, the Way is also a path we can walk. Paradoxically, it is also pathless, inasmuch as, for the mind in tune with it, there is nowhere that is not the path. But this Way will freely negate culturally conditioned assumptions, thwart ego-driven notions and ambitions, defy the consensus-persuasions of our times. And often, it is a way of *not* doing things: not acting as a self-important entity who feels separate from the rest of existence, not acting out of anxiety, or any ridiculous sense of dominance, or an endless desire for increase. Usually, more is *not* better: simplicity creates space for gain, but in having too much one just becomes confused. Ultimately, this Way empties one of false notions of self, making it possible to finally get out of the way of one's own light. Here is the way of human life where it flows most naturally: in harmony with the powerful river-current of the universal Way. In this it is the path of supreme effectiveness or efficiency, the way of operating by Dao's power, or *de*.

Three approaches to the way and its power

For those unfamiliar with Daoism, some confusion may be spared if we understand from the outset that what we now call Daoism encompasses three outwardly different kinds of practices. (It is doubtful that the Chinese of old would have made the distinctions we will look at, or even have called their natural way of thinking "Daoist," because it was not so much a distinct school of thought as a cultural way of thinking that recognized the Dao.) But the three approaches to Dao and its power share a common ground. First, they hold in common a recognition that all of existence, from the smallest speck to the vast Universe, flows, and is in fact a constant flow of interrelated energies. Second, their different practices are all based on the understanding that this flowing power or energy can be conserved or cultivated to the point where one may flow with supreme effectiveness. In other words, all three branches are expressions of the desire to live life by the power or virtue *(de)* of the Dao.[7]

Many readers will have some familiarity with a Daoist approach to health practices that seek to increase the supply of the Dao's power that it finds in the life force, or *qi*. This includes qigong (chi gung), taijiquan (tai chi chuan), and gong fu (kung fu) exercises, acupuncture for unblocking the body's energy channels, Daoist yogic cultivation, and the development of traditional Chinese medicine with its pharmacopoeia of herbs.

Second, there is a shamanic practice which comprises the major folk religion of China, and operates in some respects almost like an organized Church. Daoist priests believed the power they cultivated to be vicarious, that is, beneficial to the common folk in such phenomena as bringing much needed rain, warding off plagues, or dealing with restless ghosts. We see their understanding of the flow of *qi* in the proper design and placement of things, called *feng-shui*.

The third branch is commonly called philosophical Daoism. Although it cannot really be separated from the other two and likely never existed as some sort of separate school, it can be distinguished because it is more about the philosophy of life which teaches how to *harmonize with* and *conserve* Dao's power as it flows through human beings. It calls us toward the observation and contemplation of nature's own processes and it is the theme of this book. The primary sources for this approach to life are found in the *Dao De Jing*, the *Hua Hu Ching*, and the writings of Zhuangzi (Chuang-Tzu), and Liezi (Lieh-Tzu). We will look at some of the main themes to better understand the whole.

---

7   The differences between them are discussed here only briefly. For a richer treatment, the reader is encouraged to read the chapter on Taoism in Huston Smith's *The World's Religions*. (San Francisco: Harper San Francisco, 1991), pp. 198-207.

tian di (heaven and earth)

Interconnecting Heaven and Earth

It is not uncommon to hear various expressions of people's existential disconnection from the world, or even from existence itself. "I didn't ask to come into this world..." Even the phrase "*into this world*" implies a fundamental otherness from the world, as if we are here only by divine permission in some sort of probationary state. We have inherited from various world mythologies vague feelings that any divine realm only tolerates our existence, and must be somehow appeased to put up with us at all. For some, this is compounded by residual ideas of the inferiority or inherent evilness of matter, and such notions have scarred the collective psyche with vague feelings of unworthiness and defensiveness, even among the non-religious. There is a feeling that we just don't really belong, and need to defend our unworthy selves against the universe as foreigners in an unwelcoming land.

Daoist sensibilities are quite different from all that. Chinese terms for the world reveal a sense of connection, a feeling of *place* within the cosmos. They are terms of *belonging*, both on the Earth and within the greater cosmos. This cosmos which includes us is variously called "the ten-thousand things" (*wan wu*), or "heaven and below" (*tian xia*). There is also the inclusive phrase, "Heaven and earth" (*tian di*), and it was felt that the human being is centered between the two, as the place where the heavens and earth are merged, ideally in perfect balance. If you wanted to know the level of someone's spirituality or connection to the heavenly, you could measure it well by how he or she treats the earth, and all the ten-thousand things, plants, animals, and fellow humans. Zhuangzi considers a person seeking the heavenly while holding disdain for the earthly realm to be either mad or a charlatan. Earth is the expression of Heaven. Though the terms for the world can sometimes be interchangeable, each term has its own particular conceptual context. Hidden behind each is a feeling for the world which is not brought out completely by any word-for-word translation into English.

The "ten thousand things" (*wan wu*), could be, in modern prosaic terms, "the trillions of things," or even "countless things." Obviously, even "trillions" is not a high enough number to encompass all the varied phenomena in the Universe; it is simply high enough that we know what we mean by the phrase. For the Chinese of old, ten-thousand was a high enough number. Some translate *wan wu* as "all creatures," which is fine if we remember that this does not imply a Western idea where the Creator creates from wholly *outside* the system. This is discussed more fully under the next phrase *tian xia*. In this book *wan wu* is usually translated "the myriad things" or "the myriad creatures," because its usage seems to imply the marvelous diversity which includes not only people, but animals, plants, inanimate things, and basically the entire realm of varied material phenomena.

We will also appreciate the world as that which is "below the heavens." *Tian xia* may be translated as: "all below Heaven," or simply "the world," "the nation," "the empire," or "everyone." This phrase is often used when talking about the human realm, or societal order, but it also takes the broader view of the earthly within the context of what is greater or beyond it.

The earthly realm is more limited in both time and space than the heavens, and is in that sense "inferior" to the heavenly. Heaven was felt to be the source of order, and in that way, "superior" to earth. In "all below Heaven" *xia* can mean "below" in the sense of "inferior to" as well as spatially beneath. But the earthly is never denigrated by comparison to the heavenly. Confucius may have said, "Earth is small; heaven is great," but in the Daoist sensibilities, neither is inferior or superior because they go together inseparably. They are both necessary aspects of the Dao, and a human is a place of *integration* of earthly and heavenly. When, deep down, you come to feel the universal cosmos as your *home*, the existential angst of being here only by divine tolerance is dissolved. Co-arising with nature, *as* nature, one no longer feels estranged from existence and can no longer feel or act in a hostile manner toward nature.

"Below Heaven" refers to this observable world in which we walk, eat, and conduct our affairs. But the deep blue sky in the day and stars at night appear boundless. Earth is below Heaven, and yet it is wholly interconnected with it as one of the natural expressions of the Dao. Earth's energy is feminine, or *yin*, and that of the heavens is masculine, or *yang*, and these two polarities arise mutually. Each implies the other. To seek one to the exclusion of the other was considered foolishness and a source of destructive behavior. The earth's interconnectedness to Heaven and to the Dao is a mystery, and penetrating it is wisdom.

The third phrase, "Heaven and earth" (*tian di*), is translated by some as "above and below," or simply, "the Universe." Lest we make too much of the distinction between the phrases "Heaven and earth" and "below Heaven," different Chinese copies of the *Dao De Jing* can use the phrases interchangeably. Though heaven and earth may be distinguished through naming, they are here understood as the necessary polarities of one and the same continuum.

In Daoist thinking, opposing forces are not mutually exclusive "either/or" categories. Heaven and earth *cannot* be opposed to each other: everything is within the Dao, and heaven and earth are thus mutually interdependent and even *mutually arising*. As symbolized by the *yin-yang* image, all opposing forces are actually part of one whole – polarities in a self-balancing Universe.

Each side of the *yin-yang* diagram has a small abode in the heart of the other through which each calls for the other, because they arise mutually, like front and back, right and left, sound and silence. Zhuangzi asks, incredulously, how one can cling only to heaven and care nothing for earth! He answers that they are correlative and that to know one is to know the other. So, a "spiritually minded" person who rejects the earthly is thereby rejecting both earth and heaven. There may be many claims, in words, about one's spirituality, but one's actual spirituality is revealed in how one treats the natural world, which is the expression of heaven. As mentioned before, Zhuangzi regards anyone who seeks the heavenly while rejecting the earthly as either deceitful or crazy.[8]

In this ancient wisdom tradition, heaven includes not only that vast realm of sun, moon and stars, but also the spirits of the deceased ancestors and heroes of old. Earth is this natural world of animal, vegetable, and mineral, but also the abode of the flow of the invisible energy of *qi*, which is observable in the changing seasons, or in one's health. Weather patterns were considered events of heaven rather than earth, even though they obviously take place here and affect conditions here.

It is important that we do not confuse *tian* with a Western, Judeo-Christian heaven standing with some sort of judicial opposition over earth. Very early on, in the Shang Dynasty (from the 17–11th centuries BCE), the Chinese referred to their supreme god as *Shangdi* ("Lord on High"). During the Zhou Dynasty which followed, *tian*, became synonymous with this deity. The heavens have some sovereignty, but there is no longer a distinct deity operating *from* heaven; the ordering principle comes to be an aspect of the universe itself. And in Daoist thinking, this Universe is not seen to

---

8   Chuang-tzu xvii.5

run by the same sort of capricious authority a deity would exercise. It seems more like natural laws of equilibrium, flow, change, and processes of transformation.

Likewise, in Daoist thinking, the physical Universe does not require an *external* Prime Cause or prior creator to construct it and set things into motion. If you told them that all things must be explained in terms of a prior creator outside the system, they might ask, "Well, then, if such is necessary, who created this creator?" Western religious notions of a cosmic Monarch and Judge are not appropriate here. There is an old tradition about a First Being named Di, who is a sort of creator god (referred to in verse 4), but although all creation comes *after* Di, Dao is yet *prior* to,[9] and is the actual antecedent of all things, including Di. Dao is called the Mother of Heaven and Earth, and the Great Ancestor. Dao is the deep source out of which all comes forth. It is perfect emptiness – it is nothing, and yet it is in everything we call *something*.

Alan Watts noted back in the 1960's how Isaac Newton famously introduced a *mechanical* model of the Universe in which all we need to know can be explained in terms of mechanical laws of forces and motion. Though Newton retained the Creator of this mechanism-universe, the model led to later developments in science which felt that they got rid of any need for a Maker. The common modern view is that there is just this universe running itself mechanically according to physical laws. Yet the post-Newtonian sciences seem to have retained unconsciously a view of the Universe as if it were something *made*, that is, constructed of divisible parts which act upon each other mechanically. This is a model of the universe after a watch with no Watch-maker, running according to physical "laws" with no Law-giver. This mechanical view is prevalent in almost all the sciences of the western world. But a mechanical thing is an artifact of creation. In this sense, science is still treating the universe as a *built* thing.

Watts' point was that there are models to be considered other than the mechanical model. For example, Indian Hindu philosophy views the universe as a divine drama, the play of the Godhead. For the Chinese, the Universe is not a mechanistic relic. It is felt to be

---

9   Li Yueh, cited by Red Pine, p.9.

an organic whole, just like the organisms which grow within it.[10] The Western paradigm of seeing the Universe as *a construct* leaves us faced the wrong way in many of our notions. Rather than seeing the Universe as an assemblage of parts, the Chinese observed it as something that grows, and growing things grow *from the inside* outwards, as with a plant or a fetus, in which all so-called "parts" are already inside in the essence and co-arise, mutually interdependent. Because a brain does not survive or function without a stomach, nor a stomach without a brain, they arise together.

We observe this principle of mutually arising phenomena all through nature when something happens of itself. That something is the movement of the Dao. In the Dao, the whole cosmos *grows* everything *integrally*, including us. We come *from* the world, not *into* it as if we were space creatures or angels landing on a world alien to us.

In perceiving the Universe as an organic whole, we are closer in cosmology to the newer science of quantum physics than to the older Newtonian, or mechanistic, view of the Universe. Physicists John Gribbin and Paul Davies wrote about the new physics:

> "The old machine vocabulary of science is giving way to language more reminiscent of biology than physics – adaptation, coherence, organization, and so on....So with the machine analogy now looking distinctly strained, the link with Newtonian materialism is fading fast.[11]

Renowned physicist David Bohm once said "Physics is more like quantum organism than quantum mechanics. I think physicists have a tremendous reluctance to admit this."[12] Those who sought to cultivate Dao thousands of years ago were closer to the integral view of modern quantum physics because, of course, they

---

10 For a fuller discussion of three dominant theories of nature in the history of philosophy, see Alan Watts, *The Tao of Philosophy*: the Edited Transcripts (Rutland, Vermont: Charles E. Tuttle, 1995), pp. 20-25.

11 Paul Davies and John Gribbin, *The Matter Myth* pp. 55, 56

12 Interview with David Bohm, conducted by F. David Peat and John Briggs, published in *Omni* magazine, January 1987

had never received a Newtonian mechanistic view of the Universe. For them everything was interrelated so that one feels *continuous with* one's environment: a human is one intelligent center of the whole interplay of harmonizing forces. All of existence is dynamic, and not made of separate, static *things*. If we could conceive of the Universe without any nouns, but only with verbs, or "what is happening," we would be closer to both the Daoist and modern scientific views of reality, in which the Universe is made of interrelated dynamic *processes* rather than individual *objects*. Most people in the West still strive under the outdated mechanical view of the Universe (the "clockwork universe"). [13]

The early Asian feeling for our place in the world puts humans in direct and inescapable relation to our environment. The Universe is not felt to be an insensate artifact, whether of a prior creation or a big bang; it is still birthing and growing everything, including us, as an organic whole. It has no "parts" except through our naming them as such. Naming is dividing. When we stop mentally dividing and labeling, the Universe and the world will appear as they really are: integrated, and acting more like that which we find in our own bodies: a self-regulating, self-balancing organism with its own intelligence. The heavens grow solar systems which grow planets which grow people, plants, and animals, etc.

We ourselves are all of the same mysterious yet observable process. It does not require an external authority in charge of it any more than one's body has an organ in charge of the rest. One might claim such authority for the brain, but the brain is as utterly dependent on the stomach, heart, lungs, and endocrine system as they are on it. No one thing is actually in charge of the rest. All aspects arise mutually and the body functions *of itself*. Likewise, a cabbage does not require a builder to assemble its cells or a boss to command its absorption of water. Whatever is "in charge" is inherent in the very fabric of the cabbage, so that whatever the plant does happens *of itself*, and this is the theme of Chapter 4.

---

13 *op. cit.* For a discussion of Newtonian science and the Genesis story, see Alan Watts, *The Tao of Philosophy*, p. 20.

Much of this may seem fairly obvious, but, on reflection, our common feeling is not like this. We have been conditioned to feel that reality is separated into independent parts that must always strive with each other for survival, improvement, or management of the world, as though each being is not a legitimate expression of the Totality. We speak of "the conquest of" space or of a mountain, and of "dominion over" nature (a catastrophic misinterpretation of the Genesis story which cannot be addressed here). We fear letting things take their natural course and thus busy ourselves to control and manage the world lest it go awry for lack of our ingenuity. Laozi says:

> Some think they can manage the world through control,
> but I perceive no successful end to this.
> The world is the vessel of the Sacred
> and is not to be shoved around.
> Acting upon it only ruins it.
> Seizing it, you lose it.

Not understanding the interrelatedness of all things, we presume to improve genetics, eradicate species at will, and use resources until they are depleted. We have had dominion over air and water until they are toxic and the seas are dying; we have had dominion over food supplies until people are eating unnatural factory excretions nicely packaged. We have had dominion over animals resulting in bio-regional imbalances which brought diseases, decimation of populations, and species extinctions. Trees, which act as the lungs of our planet, are converted into packaging and advertising at a hor-rifying rate.

Tragically, this same notion of human dominion is often extended over other humans, even those in other countries, so that entire populations may be thought to need either an overthrow of their government or massive and organized killing to bring them (and usually their resources) under another's control. As Zhuangzi said, "By ethical arguments and moral principles, the most terri-ble crimes are argued to be necessary, and even of great benefit for humanity." Moving from the violent to the merely meddlesome, we also see human dominion over humans in ever-increasing laws, regulations, procedures, and legal arrangements that take precedence over the rather uncomplicated affair of living. People now spend the bulk of their lives in abstract labors unrelated to the simple business of living, in order to accumulate enough money to pay for a plot of ground on which to sit and food to eat, water to drink. It is perhaps conceivable that the propensity for division and control has put things madly out of balance.

The first step in returning to balance is a matter of rousing ourselves from erroneous views of reality. No significant change is possible without a change of vision. We can come to realize that we are *not* separate entities from the rest of the world, that the "ten-thousand things" include us, and that we all alike make up "all below Heaven." "Heaven and Earth" is ultimately *one* realm, not two, and our only chance of being saved from striving, disruption, exhaustion, nonsense and self-annihilation comes by understanding and actually feeling our place in the whole. Heaven's way, according to Laozi, is to bring forth, love, and nurture all things, but assert no dominion, to contend with none, to lead by putting others ahead, to take the lower position, to remain whole by being able to bend, and to show equanimity.

Creating separations through naming

The sages of old understood that the very act of naming gives rise to the notion and the feeling that the world is made up of completely separable things. This is like seeing a tree as made from separate parts, that is, from roots, trunk, branches, leaves, bark, pith, cells, cell-walls, *ad infinitum*, rather than what it is: an organically whole *event* comprising even the soil, air, water and sunlight. Conceptually, it might have whatever "parts" we make up in our propensity to divide, categorize, and name, but the tree remains in actuality an organic whole.

Douglas Adams quipped in *The Hitchhiker's Guide to the Galaxy*, "If you try and take a cat apart to see how it works, the first thing you have on your hands is a non-working cat." This is because a cat is something which *grows* rather than something which is *con-*

structed. Likewise, a tree is a process going on in relation to larger processes, such as the world of sunlight, air, warmth, moisture, soil, microorganisms, etc. In turn, the larger processes are going on in relation to a solar system, and so it goes, on into the vastness. The only dividing line between one "thing" and another, or even between you and the Universe at large, is the one in our heads: we *think* of things as separate, and *name* them to keep them distinct from the rest. And then there arise distinctions between "greater" and "lesser" things. As a Zenrim poem says, "In the landscape of spring, there is nothing superior, and nothing inferior. The flowering branches grow naturally: some short, some long."

Illustrative of this point is the story of when Master Dung Guo asked Zhuangzi where the *Dao* is to be found. Zhuangzi told him "Well, there's nowhere it's *not* found." When Dung Guo pressed him to be more specific, Zhuangzi pointed to an ant and said "There." Dung Guo then asked if it's also in even lesser beings. The answer, came, "It's in the weeds too." Dung Guo persisted: "Is Dao even in lesser things than that?" Zhuangzi pointed to a broken bit of tile in the dirt and declared it to also have Dao. Intrigued, Dung Guo asked him just how far down the scale of things one can go and still find Dao, to which Zhuangzi pointed to a turd, leaving Dung Guo finally speechless. But Zhuangzi went on and told him that none of his questions got at the real point of the matter, which is that what we may think of as lesser or "least" hasn't any less of *Dao*, which is great in all things, and complete in all things, because reality is *one*.

ziran (nature)

Nature as What is "of Itself So"

One of the most essential themes of the *Dao De Jing* is *wu-wei*, (not-doing) which is the efficiency of not-forcing or meddling in things. But understanding the effectiveness of non-action is predicated on a basic trust of nature, and of the principle that the most beneficial events happen spontaneously, or "of themselves." *Nature*, in Chinese, is *ziran* (often written "tzu-jan") and means "of itself so." The best action is *that which happens of itself*. Reading the *Dao De Jing* one finds the most authenticity and efficiency in the most natural events, the most spontaneous actions, that is, in what is without external contrivance or forcing.

When we observe nature, we are seeing things that happen of themselves. We observe a sort of intelligence at play continuously in phenomena such as flowers attracting bees which in turn help propagate the flowers, or thousands of starlings changing direction simultaneously, or the rhythms of the seasons, or the self-balancing fluctuations of food-chains and weather patterns. The planet has managed itself for quite a long time before the advent of technology, but so many of us have a basic mistrust of nature, as is evidenced in our desire to control genetics or people or circumstances in order to ensure what we feel will be greater success in life. In contrast with Daoist thinking, ours is a philosophy of interference and struggle, a busy and even meddlesome way of life as expressed in the motto, "Make it happen."

The Daoist sage has no interest in making things happen. For her or him, the issue is this: do we cooperate and flow with the larger reality, or do we get in the way of our own light and live in self-centered ideas of domination, control, taking, or forcing things? The former way flows *with* life and has the power of the Universe in it; the latter is an overly assertive individuated power that sort of pushes and shoves its way through life and leads to exhaustion, complications, excessive behavior, and eventually, ruin.

The scientists who study living things, namely botanists, biologists, and ecologists, have for a long time realized that there is no way to really study any organism in isolation; an organism can be understood only *in reference to* and *in the context of* its environment. Likewise, the Daoists of old understood that we are integrally connected, or interconnected, with the earth. We may not be rooted like trees, but we are nonetheless the fruit of this planet. We can perceive the world precisely because our nature *is* earth nature: our senses arise with and are attuned to the environment from which they grew.

One brought up in western religion might challenge, "Are we not also spiritual beings, or at least supposed to be?" A Daoist might be puzzled by the question, because for her or him the earthly and the spiritual are not thought of as so separate as they are in the west. The earthly is an expression of the heavenly, and both the earthly and the heavenly are the varied expression of – or manifestation of – the Dao. Rather than seeing heavenly and earthly as opposed, or the spiritual and material as in conflict, we find them integral to each other, and the perfect human being is one in whom heaven and earth mingle perfectly. The Universal Way permeates everything and flows out to the furthest reaches of the Universe, encompassing all, including humanity. Going from the smaller to the greater, humanity emulates Earth, Earth emulates the heavens, the heavens emulates the Way, and the Way emulates itself.

The interconnectedness of Dao with all things forms the basis for life. When one realizes that one belongs *with* everything else, there is no feeling that one can survive only by possessing, laying claim, or forcing things. Dao gives birth to all things without lording over them, nourishes all things without laying claim. It does not "act upon" things, yet leaves nothing undone. When all is seen as one self-balancing continuum, there is no need for friction or wrestling, no need for assertions or demands. Perhaps that is why in Daoism there are no commandments, no threats, and no persnickety moralism. Because the Way nurtures all things equally, it is honored or reverenced spontaneously. Its power or virtue (*de*) is both the nourishing essence of the physical world and the grace of life that recognizes Dao. In our right minds, we enjoy a natural reverence that is neither commanded nor sanctimonious. It is spontaneous.

Verse 51 of the *Dao De Jing* says the Dao gives birth to the ten-thousand things and its power (*de*, or virtue) nourishes them. Materiality gives them form, and their functions within the whole complete that form (they evolve in adaptation to, and cooperation with, their environment). Here, all things, *as they are naturally*, are already "at home" in the universe and honor Dao. Commandments would be otiose and spoil the sense of harmony.

For now, let us bracket the belief that everything will go wrong if left to itself, and that people will become robbers or rapscallions if they are not controlled by authorities. Imagine another possibility, namely, that there is a way to govern people with neither meddling nor force. There is a saying that a government governs best which governs least. The *Dao De Jing* affirms a similar principle, asserting that the superior ruler (that is, the *most effective* ruler) governs by *not* interfering in people's lives. In verse 17 it is suggested that with the best rulers, the people are barely aware of their presence. Next best are those who are loved and praised. Worse are those who are feared, and the worst are those who are despised. It is a faithless ruler who finds no one faithful, and a deceptive ruler who has to use political rhetoric. The sagely ruler is quite different: unassertive and sparing of words, the best ruler completes his work and the people are under the impression that they did it themselves, spontaneously, or *naturally*.

All of life takes on a lighter, more natural and less anxious quality for the person who trusts Heaven and earth and is sensitive to our connection to them. Not everything will go as we want. Tragedies occur, we wear out, our accomplishments may be short lived, but our identification is with Dao as a whole rather than with a notion of an isolated self. We find ourselves in resonance with reality. Things change, Dao only is eternal. With which do we identify ourselves?

Heraclitus said, "Existence flows." Laozi emphasizes that existence flows *spontaneously – zi* (or *tzu*). There really is nothing that is improved or gained by trying to stop the spontaneity of Nature through clinging, controlling, or capturing. One may enjoy a refreshing breeze while it is happening *of itself*, but capture it in a box to enjoy later and lo! It's no longer a breeze. Recognizing this, the wisest, in acting for good in the world, always prefer what is authentic, arising naturally, and enjoy it as it happens. They do not cling to what is not eternal, and thus also find no reason for meddling or using force. Often when we act upon something we diminish it. Anxiously grasping we lose hold. Pin a butterfly and the flying is lost. A person identified with the Way does not act upon things and thus does not ruin them, does not seek to control things and thus does not lose.

It is not that the sage sits around doing nothing all day. It is that his or her undertakings do not seek to control, manipulate, or interfere with the natural state of things. To live this way presupposes a shift of consciousness away from society's conditioned thinking (being told what to desire) and toward the natural order of things in harmony with the Dao. Thus the only thing the sage holds to is freedom from erroneous desires, from mind which seeks to grasp, from the egoistic delusion of wanting more and more and more. The person of Dao does not want something just because it is rare or difficult to obtain. Cultivating Dao within, there is no disquiet over external treasures. The Treasure – Dao – is within, there is no need to seek approval or follow convention. What a person of Dao teaches others is the art of *unlearning* our conditioning so that we may return to what we have lost sight of or missed altogether: our inner connection to the natural world at large, and to the Dao which brings forth and nourishes all things. In helping people return to what arises of itself, to *the self-so*, the sage cannot dare to act upon others.

zi (of itself)

Trusting the Spontaneous and Uncontrived

If nature is that which is "of itself so," authentic human nature is also that which arises of itself. Similar to the concept of *ziran*, there is just *zi*, which encompasses meanings such as *itself, of itself, themselves*, or *of its own accord*. It also means *spontaneously*. When something acts of itself without any external coercion, nor from social convention, it is acting according to its true nature. This does not mean just doing "my thing, my way" as some sort of defiance of societal rules. Even doing one's own thing may come from our little, constricted, egoistic sense of self. This still leaves one stranded from one's true nature, inasmuch as one's "own thing" expresses some socially programmed value. For minds conditioned by societal artifice, it is quite possible to follow pre-programmed internal processes without following what is true or natural.

What is this spontaneity which unfolds from something higher than cultural conditioning? Life unfolds "of itself." As it does, it doesn't make mistakes. Following cultural programming, people often try to do good things, but coming from the wrong place, these actions result in further complications, unintended consequences, unfulfilling results, or an artificial sort of goodness. Notice that the things we most want from people – love, loyalty, caring, etc. – are only truly valuable when they are spontaneous rather than calculated. Commanding someone to love makes a parody of love. Trying too self-consciously to be good makes one a goody-goody. All the efforts of the constricted egoistic sense of self just get in the way of one's own light.

On the other hand, when we act according to our true nature, we are not forcing anything, and may not even be self-conscious about our action. This is acting *with* nature; as such, it seems a sort of non-action because there is effortlessness. This is called *wu-wei*, and refers to that unforced, uncalculating kind of activity which is, ultimately, the Dao acting through you. *Wu-wei* is not a self-conscious, deliberately taken action. It is doing without "do-ership." Yet with it, nothing essential remains undone.

Everything in the natural Universe happens in such a way. Seasons find their rhythm, rain waters seeds, sunlight warms and energizes them, and all the rest, but is it "being done" by something? When one's heart is beating, is one *acting* to make it happen? If not, then, who is? The question is silly because there is no self-conscious *who*; it happens *zi*, of itself, naturally. This simple concept is key. Here, the good life has to do with uncontrived action, naturalness, spontaneity, and non-striving. Surprisingly, this leads to pure effectiveness and the ending of anxiety.

Is this just a pleasant fantasy? In the *Dao De Jing* this natural spontaneity is considered integral to good government. A ruler in spiritual union with the Dao does not need to act upon things. The Dao never "acts upon" anything, and yet nothing remains undone (verse 37). Laozi affirms that if princes and kings could hold to this, all things would naturally transform themselves, and the world will naturally (*zi*) settle into peace.

Things must settle into peace *naturally* because enforced peace is not true peace, just as a democracy imposed on others would not, by definition, be a democracy. Dao does not work by imposing, forcing, commanding, or threatening: it *has no use for* authority. This is why Dao can always assume the lower place, the smaller place. As small as nothingness, it can penetrate anywhere; yielding as water, it cannot be harmed. It does not stand out as special or make a name for itself. Being nameless, simple, and small it does not interfere with anything, yet is the natural order of everything.

The Way is forever nameless. It should not be another -*ism*, even though we like to call this approach "Daoism." It evokes no compulsion to follow it religiously. The Dao does not require that anyone follow it at all. As with a river-current one may choose to swim with it or assert life against it. Like water, Dao follows the lower places and trickles into the small places. One might be reminded of Jesus' words about being the servant of all.

Like the invisible quanta of energies hidden beneath space-time and yet integral to all material objects, Dao can be called infinitesimal, and its virtue runs inexhaustibly through everything in the world. It is silent, invisible, intangible, yet nothing has power over it. If rulers governed by this principle, says Laozi, all things would yield of their own accord (*zi*). In this vision, Heaven and earth are united in harmony in the spirit of the sagely ruler, with the result that the virtue of Dao descends like a "sweet dew" on all alike. Peace and concord come, not by any decree, but by following our original simplicity and moving with the Way.

Our conventional wisdom tells us governing requires authority and control. But Laozi does not teach effectiveness through domination, or righteousness by threat, or fixing situations through violence, or improving anything by asserting ourselves over it. The *Dao De Jing* is not conventional thinking. It even assumes the only kind of person who could govern *well* would be one *given over to the cultivation of wisdom*. Political mastery here depends on spiritual mastery. A "sage" is a person of such depth of understanding and deep connection that even his or her meditative presence can enable an unruly people to find order and settle into it. To the mind that is still, the whole Universe surrenders. This sounds to Western ears like magical fantasy, but it speaks of the power of flowing only with what is ultimately real and enduring. A sage is one who is unobstructed, or transparent to the natural flow and order of the Universe. When a true sage governs, Dao and its virtue (power) is channeled to the people. Thus he finds that when he takes *no action* (*wu wei*) the people transform *themselves*. While he enjoys quietude, the people correct *themselves*; when he doesn't meddle, the people prosper *by themselves*, and since he isn't driven by ambition and desire, the people become pure and simple within themselves.

That such a state, or such a *State*, could be possible is not a point that can be argued; one either accepts it or does not. But to seers such as Laozi, the Buddha, Jesus of Nazareth, and even Gandhi, the way to transform any society was through being transformed oneself. This means that in following what the Buddha called the Dharma, what Jesus called the kingdom of Heaven, and what Laozi called Heaven's Way, we rely on something greater than our ability to act on the world. The sage notices that "Heaven's Way does not fight, yet is excellent at winning; it does not speak, yet is excellent in answering; it is not summoned, yet appears *on its own* (*zi*); is never anxious, yet plans excellently. Heaven's net is vast and it is wide-meshed, yet nothing slips past it" (verse 73).

All the above expresses a fundamental trust in the Universe as something that brings everything into being and also harmonizes Nature's interrelations. The virtue of the Dao is observable in the many things in the world which function of themselves. The heart-beat speeds or slows appropriately on its own. Our bones grew from infancy to adulthood, but we don't know how we do it; it happens of itself. Both outside and inside our bodies, we observe the processes of Nature. We are each an aspect of its processes, though we too often feel as if we are separate entities. Feeling this way, and experiencing Nature as if it were a foreign object in our subjective world, we would like to control it, but Nature is that which is *of itself so*, and it includes each of us. We are not separate.

Lu Nung-shih (a Daoist scholar, 1042 - 1102) said, "Something is natural when nothing can make it so, and nothing can make it not so." The idea that we should continually improve what is natural is, for the Daoist, a confused interference with life. We are not out-side of nature; we *are* nature; we *are* what is happening of itself. The feeling that we have to master ourselves or dominate nature is a sort of schizophrenia, a split that puts us out of accord with the *Way* of things, muddying the waters, so we act out of confusion and strife.

Rejecting the systematic striving prevalent in society, we return to the innocence of one who does not feel separate from the "self-so." This is the only possibility for quietude and a new way of acting in this world. Frenetic striving and perpetual conquering, controlling, and taking is not properly cured through arguments or legislation. Ultimately, the cure comes through recognizing the fundamental state of existence as inherently intelligent and trustworthy when left in balance. All true change, deep change, comes through a fundamental change in our view of reality, our recognition of "what is."

Learned behaviors and culturally-conditioned values typically lead away from our Source. As Laozi says, "The further one goes, the less one knows." There is no satisfying end on the Road to More except the dead end – death undoes the accumulations of learning and possessions. Yet there seems to be no end to activity directed at attaining these things. Laozi sees as delusional all our actions which affirm conquest above gentleness, nervous activity above stillness, accumulation above divesting, or the glittery and showy over the substantial.

So Laozi asks whether we might return to the stillness which allows our mental "muddied water" to settle and let our spirit become clear again. That is the only mind/heart out of which authentic and helpful actions arise. Verse 15 asks whether we can remain unmoving until the right action arises of itself. That is, can we bring into action only what comes from the clarity of inner stillness? This brings us to the next key theme of the *Dao De Jing*: the appropriate kind of action. The sage, the person of highest character, is one whose actions are *wu wei*, a phrase which suggests the highest success comes through the effortlessness of harmony with life's natural processes.

wu-wei (not doing)

The Power of Emptiness

Confucianism succeeded for over two millennia in providing a model for social harmony by relying on intricate social conventions and ritualized behavior. Daoists found such behavior overly complicated and artificial, and were dubious of anything that made people lose their natural spontaneity. Freedom in life comes from a free mind; tranquility in life comes from a tranquil mind; unencumbered life comes from an unencumbered mind. And these were all that is needed for society to get on well.

We find that the life-style of a person of Dao arises primarily from a type of intelligence in which one's actions flow naturally, easily, and thus, most effectively. By analogy, one might think of using the wind to sail the waters instead of grunting and exerting oneself against the currents by brute force. The principle of efficient action is also used in certain martial arts such as soft-style gong fu, taijiquan, judo, and aikido. In each of these, instead of struggling with force against force, one overcomes opposition with minimal force or effort by flowing *with* an opponent's energy until it can be redirected, often using the opponent's own force to lead him effortlessly to the ground (or hurled away!).

This peculiar kind of action in life is a major theme in the *Dao De Jing*. We are speaking of an effortless and even egoless action which results in the supreme effectiveness and efficiency of being in harmony with the Universe's creative flow. The short phrase which describes this effortless action is *wu wei*, and, though it occurs many times, it is somewhat enigmatic. The first word, *wu*, has a common meaning of "no," "not," or "non-" and a more specialized meaning having to do with the nothingness out of which everything arises.

Wei commonly means do, act, or work. In most translations *wu wei* is rendered as something like "not doing" or "not acting." The other use of *wu* as no-thing-ness must also be considered here, so that the phrase suggests acting from a spirit of *wu*, or acting only out of a particular state of mind which is empty of a self-conscious "doer." Various translations of *wu wei* include such phrases as empty-action, not forcing, or taking no unnatural action. Its meaning becomes clearer by the examples of its use in the *Dao De Jing*.

Wu wei as a sort of emptiness-action makes more sense out of the odd phrase *wei wu wei*, which appears to be saying "do not-doing," but it can also be thought of as something like "act with emptiness-action," that is, actions empty of self-consciousness, contrivance, meddling, force, or excessive calculation. When our sense of self is too heavy our actions are felt to be of a separate order from the rest of existence. They become I-versus-It actions and lead to more trouble. But when one acts from a state of no-self, without a sense of being *the doer*, then the action is felt as arising from something indefinable – that same hidden essence out of which all events in the Universe arise. Dis-identified with the ego, actions arise from the universal stillness of Dao, the same way everything else in the Universe does.

Wu-action is not performed in search of recognition or reward, and is not balled up in anxiety over a particular outcome. The meanings of *wu wei* and *wei wu wei* cannot be derived fully from a dictionary-definition approach. The meanings must be intuited to some degree from the contexts in which they are used. So we can start with a look at *wu wei* in verse two, where I have translated it in a way which I hope will convey the meaning of "not putting things in opposition" that is, not striving. When we are free of the mental habit of opposing things (such as difficult/easy, long/short, or high/

low), and see them as going *with* each other, then our minds do not live in the friction of dualities, and we naturally cease striving for this against that. Laozi infers that what we typically consider conflicting opposites are really harmonized opposites; that is, they arise mutually as the necessary ends of one system.

So, in verse 2 the old master offers examples: Being and non-being give rise to each other, difficult and easy complete each other, long and short define each other, high and low depend on each other. For music, the tones and intervals require each other to make melody. Back follows front. In each of these cases, what we feel are opposed to each other are seen to define each other, even to require each other. Yin and yang play together; they make love, as the male and the female energies. So, the sage does not push for one side to win: more is not better than less, up is not better than down, and a wise person finds little reason to meddle with things. Even well-intended solutions often contain the seeds of new complications and problems. If you want to see the natural environment restored, *stop doing.* Then it has a chance to heal itself. Nature acts *ziran*; its power to create and balance ecosystems is inherent within itself. The person of Dao sees the myriad things arise without having to start them. And when he does act, it is without expectations. When ends are met there is no one dwelling on achievement. When nothing is clung to, nothing is lost.

We could say that with *wu wei,* one acts without opposing things to each other. We need not oppose being and non-being, high and low, etc. The context suggests an approach to life that does away with antagonisms and sees the actual harmony inherent in so-called opposites. But when we feel that light is good and dark evil, or that life is good and death bad, we adopt anxiety and strive to insure one side wins against the other.

Likewise the Daoist philosopher Zhuangzi taught that when we do something, we should remain free of attachment, forgetful of results, ignorant of ideas of profit. In this way we find Dao working through us. Sages observe that natural actions, attuned to the flow of life, have happier results, and that things go awry when even well-intentioned actions are too contrived, forced, or results-oriented.

In verse 38, we read: "A person of superior virtue does not act [*wu wei*], and does not act deliberately" (or "with ulterior motives"). There is an old Chinese saying that when the wrong person uses the right means, the right means work in the wrong way. Let us say that the person ignorant of their connection to the whole, the "separated self," is this "wrong person." When that ego-illusion disappears, there is in its place a holistic sensation, namely, that one's own actions are the very actions of the whole big picture. Empty of egocentric self, one could feel with Laozi, "My actions arise from the Universe itself."

Can there be an act without one who is acting? If our first answer is to say, "No, of course not!" then let's have a closer look. Nature is very active. But we are not accustomed to thinking of a tree "acting" or "doing something" when it grows. Empty of "doers" of the actions, any of Nature's actions are *ziran*, that is, happening "of itself." Growth, bending with the wind, or dropping seed or fruit are all actions, but not those of a "doer." Likewise, weather is very active, but empty of any self-conscious doer. Perhaps this is what Jesus hinted at when he explains the Spirit-driven life to Nicodemus: "The wind [*pneuma*, which is also "spirit"] blows where it will, and you hear the sound of it, but you don't know from where it blows or where it's going. So is everyone who has been born of the Spirit" (John 3:8). The person of spirit does not act from pre-established knowledge, that is, "knowing *from where it blows*" and is unattached to results, or "knowing *where it's going*," but flows with something indefinable and beyond one's conscious controlling. Laozi would agree: "The best traveler makes no fixed plans."

Does Nature, which acts "of itself," lack in getting things done? No. And yet it is not "acting" or "doing" in the sense we commonly feel, in order to accomplish its works. Nature acts without artifice or struggle, without "managing things," without forcing, without self-consciousness, without putting forth effort, without seeking recognition, and is thus empty of "doership." This is the sort of action that is "non-action" or *wu-wei*.

Nature acts *wu wei*, and thus acts in accordance with *the* Way. With all its seeming randomness and unsymmetrical shapes, nothing is out of order and nothing is left undone. The wind blows where it will…and so does anyone who has been born of the Spirit. Again the issue of trust arises in the Western mind: How can I get where I need to get without asserting myself over things? What is missing is a basic understanding of the Universe, of Nature, as integral and self-creative and reliable. We have been brought up to believe in a blind, stupid, dangerous Universe. In the East, it is an inherently sensible, creative universe.

The actions of the person of Dao are simply manifestations of the energies of the Universe. The Universe's actions include spinning galaxies, orbiting systems of planets, growing trees, industrious ants, and of course, ourselves. The false sense of being separate from the rest of existence erects a mental movie screen with *an image of ourselves* between us and the Universe. And we think the actions come from the screen image, the false self. Then we act from this separation anxiety, and assert ourselves over nature and others. There are no truly good actions that arise out of this illusion. It is not the troubled mind which fixes anything, but mind in tune with the universal Dao, the Way of Nature.

Following the Way essentially depends on the realization that one is *not* discontinuous with the Way. *Wu wei* eludes many because it isn't realized through arguments or persuasion. It is better realized by simply "sitting quietly with the Universe" until we realize that our separation is *mental* and nothing else. All things arise from the Source, transform, and then return to the Source. Physics has finally discovered that it is the universal background void that produces all the manifest particles of atomic physics. Mass comes from something fundamentally massless. The "emptiness" gives birth to the manifest worlds, or, as Laozi would say, "The Dao gives birth to all things. Its power nourishes them, matter gives them form, and their inclinations complete them." Contemplating yourself as *continuous with* this universal Dao is the first step toward any significant changes in your life, and a prerequisite for acting in *wu-wei*.

The Way of the sage is to govern by emptying minds of unnatural notions, loosening complications, opening the way for people to act spontaneously. Of course, the sages were not under the peculiar notion that the natural world cannot be trusted, or that spontaneity leads to chaos. Nature, after all, spontaneously balances and orders itself. What puts things out of balance is not nature, but the desire for more and more of something we have declared "good" and the actions to eradicate things we call "bad." But the sage governs in a way quite different from this. Acting with *wu wei*, nothing gets shoved out of order.

Imagine a region governed with non-interference. The people are allowed a freedom that comes through simplicity, avoiding unnatural ordinances and excessive punishments. The sages of this Way felt that the only way to consistently govern the world is by not meddling with it; as soon as one becomes busy meddling, one is thereby insufficient to govern (verse 48).

Verse 57 is even more specific in denying our conventional thinking: The more restrictive the taboos, the poorer the people; the greater the weapons, the darker the State; the more ingenious the technology, the more bizarre things are made, the more laws and decrees, the more people are made criminals. So, the sage says, "I take no action, and the people transform themselves; I enjoy quietude, and the people correct themselves; I don't meddle, and the people prosper by themselves; I don't desire, and the people become pure and simple of themselves."

The statement of the sage above, "I take no action," is "I *wu wei*"—and the people correct themselves and prosper and all is as it should be. This goes against most of our theories of success and economics and the necessity of ever-increasing laws, and many are likely to reject it out of hand as an ideal that would never work "in the real world." But it did work, with historical veracity, under the leadership of Emperor Gaozu of Han, who inaugurated the four hundred year Han dynasty (200 BCE to 200 CE) after the people had long suffered under a repressive and over-regulated Qin Dynasty. Gaozu *abolished all laws but three*. Peace and prosperity *increased*. The next year one of his governors went to govern the state of Qi, (a vast region of seventy cities) and selected an old Daoist to be his chief adviser. The governor was advised to *do nothing* and just give the people a rest from excessive authority. In the nine years of his "rule" the people prospered dramatically and his administration was considered the most successful in the empire.

Government by *wu wei* also proved successful in 179 BCE under the Emperor Wendi and Empress Dou. Taking Laozi's approach, the pair set about abolishing excessively cruel laws as well as taxes on interstate commerce. Land taxes were also reduced to the lowest necessity, a mere thirtieth of the produce. Warfare was abhorred and avoided as much as was possible.[14] This reign was considered one of the most successful in China's history.

Intelligent ease is able to conquer brute force. What is without substance eventually overcomes the substance of things. Water flows effortlessly around formidable stones. Verse 43 builds on the insight that the Dao is soft and yielding as water, affirming that "what is most soft and yielding in the world races easily over the hard things of this world; and what doesn't even have substance penetrates where there are no spaces." Here is a vivid picture of relying on the invisible, silent, intangible hidden essence of all things, and the benefit of *not-striving*, and living a teaching beyond words. It is something few in the world understand.

Wu wei is a radically different, paradoxical approach to success in life. Here one values the weaker rather than the stronger, the simple rather than the complicated, less rather than more, the yielding rather than the rigid, naturalness rather than artifice. Not feeling oneself to be "up against" the rest of existence, one is no longer suspicious of nature or of spontaneity. Simply put, one ceases striving, both psychologically and socially. Inasmuch as "the Universe is not required to be in perfect harmony with human ambition" (Carl Sagan), we might consider acting the other way around, letting our ambition be to harmonize with the Universe.

Acting without "acting," without artifice, force, or over-controlling, is not a practice to be implemented like a program of self-improvement. That itself would be artifice and "doing." Rather, *wei wu wei* arises out of a new way of perceiving the world. Any new way of living, if it is to be authentic and escape hypocrisy, must arise out of a new vision of reality. One must come to a fundamental trust of the natural Universe and its inherent intelligence, and have a feel

14 See *Tao, the Watercourse Way*, by Alan Watts and Chung-liang Al Huang, pp. 84-86.

for our place in it, indeed, feel ourselves *as* it, before one can act *wu wei*. Our actions become gentler, more fluid, more at ease. We do not act "against" anything; success in the Dao is not a matter of tension, unnatural disciplines, or "working" things; the Dao flows *of itself*.

"*Wei wu wei*," *or* "acting without acting," is the supreme effectiveness of living from a place of quietude. When problems arise and tempt us toward furious activity, a Daoist would likely advise no action until the mind is calm and the right action arises of itself. Then it is *the Dao's action*; and it comes from emptiness. Such action will not be violent, contrived, exhausting, or come to naught prematurely. Forced actions are not right actions. Right actions arise from the Universal creative principle, the Dao. That is why the sage *"does nothing, yet nothing is left undone."*

There is obviously a kind of faith operating here. We resist it because we think the Dao is far off from our personal lives and problems and that we are only reaching for it, and must do something to *attain* it. But in reality, we are not separate from "the whole of existence." Are you really some kind of a second Reality? That is the fiction of the self-conscious "doer." The power manifesting the entire Universe vibrates unseen right in one's eyebrows; it is manifesting all the sub-atomic particles as vibrating quantum probability waves billions of time every second; the Dao is as close as the ant, the weeds, the turd, the cypress tree in the garden, the tea in front of you, and *you*. It is complete in all and not lesser in anything: you're it.

sheng-ren (sage)

6
The Sage

What is herein translated as "sage" is from the Chinese *sheng ren*, which is a term which needs some explanation. *Ren* (or *jen*) is simply a human. The word *sheng* is made from the characters for a mouth, an ear, and a person standing on the earth. It is like a picture of one listening to heaven and speaking on earth. It is the term used for the Daoist adept, so perhaps it suggests a person listening to, or attuned to, the Dao in meditative repose. From its various uses in the *Dao De Jing*, is it apparent that *sheng ren* is more than simply a good person, a holy one, or wise one. While good, holy, and wise may be true, the term is used for describing one who transcends the everyday world within the everyday world.

The *sheng ren* is someone who fully embodies the Dao in thought, speech, and action, making her or him somewhat analogous to a Buddha or a Christ, except that it is not limited to any one historical figure. I translated it as "the sage" or "a sage." A sage abides daily in the virtue or power of the Dao by meditatively embracing it and transmuting it into all thoughts and activities. The sage is not entranced by cultural ideals, acquisition, excessive erudition, or unnatural behavior because the Dao is the sage's only source and only aim in life. This results in such a powerful presence that, even sitting in quietude, he or she can bring the whole political realm into order and peace.

Though the *sheng ren* is a "holy man" in the common religious use of that phrase, here it has to do more with wisdom than saintliness or sanctimony, and is not gender-specific. It could be capitalized to call attention to the fact that this is a wise person beyond the ordinary sense of the word, but I leave it uncapitalized because any sage appears to be the most ordinary of humans, except that he or she is *so natural* as to be, in society, unusual.

In Daoist writings one finds it taken for granted that the best political ruler would be one who has a high degree of wisdom and spiritual expertise. Much of the *Dao De Jing* reads as advice to people in government.[15] The sage governs in accordance with the Dao, the result being that the people are at peace, free, and enjoy life harmoniously. This kind of harmony does not come through leaders caught in the trap of attachments and fears, or a need to dominate, control, or take from others, or who are motivated merely by political ambition or a love of prestige, legacy, or power. To this day, nations suffer under such leaders. For want of wisdom and altruism, too much of the world continues in strife and destruction, led by those who can never be satisfied with what is enough. The sage is free of this sickness. Her peace and wholeness become the realm's peace and wholeness.

The cumulative picture is that a sage is a very high order of being who is at the same time utterly natural and human. She or he appears from the outside to be so ordinary as to not stand out at all. By worldly standards, the sage may appear useless, poor, or even a simpleton! But embodying Dao's virtue [*de*], she or he is a priceless gem in a poor person's coarse cloth. Inwardly there is such transparency to the flowing of Dao that, just sitting meditatively and doing nothing, the sage finds nothing left undone, and the people prosper and do what is peaceable *of themselves*. There is our word *zi* again! The reader may find it improbable that the spiritual state of the leader can have such an affect on the realm, but such is the portrayal here of the power or virtue of the sage's inward habitat.

---

15 I often wish it were required reading for anyone aspiring to any political office today!

Centered in the still-point, one lives in the timeless and limitless Dao, the infinite ground of all that happens phenomenally.

So we find that the sages are those who are unobstructed by self-concern and have wholly embraced the "Way of Heaven." Here is a brief "composite sketch" of their order of being. These enigmatic oddballs, the sages, reject the outer and hold to the inner; reject the erudition that endlessly splits things into this-versus-that, and perceive the undivided. Thus, they are a unifying and harmonizing presence in the world. Not standing in their own light they shine clearly; not self-righteous they are respected; never boasting they have real merit; not self-approving they lead. They put themselves last yet end up in front; are not self-concerned yet always preserved; forget themselves yet find their purposes realized; compete with no one, so no one can compete with them.

They avoid extravagance, showiness, or too much talk. They don't go or look anywhere else in order to understand, and don't strive in order to accomplish. They take no action, and people transform themselves. They don't meddle or interfere, as they desire neither gain nor recognition. They never act in a big, showy way nor try to accomplish great exploits. What they do, they do for others. They act without claiming merit and don't dwell on accomplishments. They treat the unkind with kindness and the deceitful with truthfulness, so that kindness and truthfulness spread. With all that, they have no self-image, and so have no desire to be seen as virtuous; doing good, they do not know it as good.

de (virtue, power)

The Power of the Dao in Personal Life

The little word "*de*" in the title *Dao De Jing* is usually translated "virtue" or "power." *Virtue* is a good translation if it is understood in the old sense of the word, as in the healing "virtue" of certain plants, medicines, etc. There are occasions where *de* translates well as virtue in the sense of goodness, but it should not be confused with the moralistic sense in which many think of virtue today. It is "good" because it brings benefit to the world. *De* is the Dao at work, so it is goodness inasmuch as a person of *de* is adept at living in harmony with the dynamic flow of the universal Dao. Goodness in this sense has nothing to do with societal conventions, and has everything to do with living in understanding of and harmony with the Way. The Chinese character's most common translations include: power, virtue, success, effectiveness, integrity, and goodness. So "goodness" here must be seen in light of the other translations: it describes living by the supreme effectiveness of harmony with the natural Universe, and unity with the unnameable, ungraspable reality underlying everything.

Where *Dao* is more elusive, *de* is more evident; it is what we can practice or cultivate. This outworking virtue of the Dao, which manifests the One in all the myriad things, is always right here, close at hand, though invisible. *De* might be compared to sunlight, which, chasing we do not get closer to, and running away, we do not get further from. We live by the dao's virtue whether we recognize it or not. But we only experience its fullness through pursuing Dao's emptiness!

De in the philosophical daoism of the *Dao De Jing*

In the *Dao De Jing* we come to the word *de* first in the final character of verse 10, as a summary description of a certain mode of being in the world. Laozi says, "In caring for the people and governing the state can you avoid using cleverness and artifice? Within activity and stillness can you hold to the role of the female? With discernment penetrating the four directions can you renounce knowing? Giving life and nurturing – giving life without possessing; acting without claiming results, leading without dominating – all these describe deep *virtue [de]*."

Supreme, all-embracing virtue follows from Dao alone, or, we might say, it is revealed only when Dao is followed. Its actions are of supreme effectiveness, inasmuch as *it is the Dao in movement*, yet Dao acts from perfect emptiness. This, of course, is a profound paradox. How is it that the empty Dao becomes the world of things? This is said to be shrouded in mystery – the mystery in which material fullness arises from the intangible. This eludes us, but in the mysterious center of Dao lies the imprint of possibility – potential. From the void of Tao come the particles of materiality.

A similar principle is described in modern particle physics as well. What was previously thought to be "empty" space-time is now understood as a plenum of quantum activity in which energies give rise to mass and matter. Similarly, the sages of old seem to have intuited a hidden, obscure Source, and in it, a *vital force*, something veritable, which is inherent in all things. By this vital force, the Universe continually manifests, creating out of nothing. Theologians called this *creatio ex nihilo* (creation out of nothing), describing something only God could do. Old science responded with *ex nihilo, nihil fit*, or "out of nothing, nothing comes." But the latest cosmologies and understanding of physical forces at the atomic and subatomic level recognize that what used to be called "empty space" or the background "void" is actually the decisive locus originating the manifestations of a physical world. So in returning to the Source, we follow *that from which everything* comes even though it is an obscure, silent, invisible, and intangible Source.

One with the source, one needn't use force.

In harmony with the Dao, one does not act out of insistence or force. Following what comes of itself, conflicts are dissolved by the fundamental integral wholeness of things. In pursuing Dao, even the internal, psychological conflicts will dissolve as notions of being a separate self fade away. In this life, *de* operates in the freedom of no-self. Rather than standing in the way of our own light (identification with a self-asserting "I"), one is identified with Dao and its outworking power, even when that power appears weak or unassertive. Quietude is strength, not weakness. "To be of few and quiet words is to be natural," says Laozi. "High winds do not last all morning, heavy rains might not last a day. If Heaven and earth do not persist, how much less the works of man. So, in daily life, one devoted to the Way becomes one with the Way; one devoted to its power becomes one with its power." (verse 23).

Dao's power is *non*-assertive; it operates without introducing notions of authority or illusions of control. It is found in the soft, the supple, the quiet places rather than in the hard, self-asserting, dominating enterprises of the world. Society may aspire to force, power, dominion, control, self-assertion, acquisition, and the high places. The reason all these eventually die out is because they are not in accord with *Dao*. The supreme effectiveness of the universal way is found, surprisingly, in *wu*, or what is *not* there. It may be described as the power of receptivity, quietude, yielding, no-self, non-interference, low places, and non-meddling. The twenty-eighth verse encourages us to "Know the masculine but hold to the feminine" and thus be like a verdant river-valley in the world. The river valleys are the low places water pursues naturally, and are thus the most lush with growth. As long as we act as the lower, the "virtue which endures" does not depart, and we enter a place of suppleness and newness.

In the same way, we are advised to "Know the bright but hold to the dark, and be a guiding example for the world." Eschewing the glare of fame and acquisition, we are more interested in being an example of return to the quiet, subdued, intangible Source. Holding to that, we do not stray from the virtue which endures. Not straying from Dao's own outworking power, we "return to the boundless." Likewise, we are encouraged to "know the glorious but hold to the lowly," and in this valley-like mode we find all our sufficiency in the virtue which endures, and "return to original simplicity."

Original simplicity

Why the quest back toward simplicity, toward the Origin? Because the Origin creates living, flowing, organically developing expressions of its power. Note the flowing striations in a block of wood. When this original creation is cut up, it is for shaping into mere tools. "But the sage makes the Uncarved his chief official – a great ruler does not split things unnaturally." Here, the chief officials in all their finery and tinkling jade are seen as mere tools, carved unnaturally so they no longer represent or express their Original Simplicity.

In the same way, a person of Dao does not split her or his actions from the operation of *de*, as in the feeling "*I* am *doing* virtue" or "I am *making* success." *De* is not a matter of arduously following rules; it flows from Dao alone. Virtue "as either contrived or prescribed is not genuine *de*."[16] The *supreme virtue* is the flow of the Way, as in nature, and is not an achievement. A person of *de* may not even be particularly religious, may have no interest in conventional rules of conduct, and not feel virtue to be a discipline, because she or he is not self-conscious about it. There are no selfless actions that come out of preoccupations with a self. No matter how noble such actions may seem, we find on reflection that they are ultimately for the furtherance or aggrandizement of a self-image.

This brings us to the theme of the 38th verse, which could be called "the virtue verse." Here *de* makes the most sense as virtue in the sense of "goodness." It begins with a cryptic sentence which, word for word, is something like: "highest virtue not virtue, therefore virtue; inferior virtue not let-go-of virtue, therefore not virtue."

How do we make sense of that? Verse 38 is describing a virtue that is unselfconscious and thus true. A person of superior virtue is not "being virtuous" and thus has true virtue. A person of inferior virtue cannot let go of being virtuous and, so, lacks true virtue.

---

16 Alan Watts, *Tao, the Watercourse Way*, p. 106.

The verse goes on to say that a person of superior virtue does not act on things, and is not purpose-driven, and that the course of inferior virtue usually leads to the need to force things. When our sense of the Way is lost, we resort to ideas of "being virtuous." Then this degenerates to a pretense of benevolence, which degenerates to moralistic self-righteousness, which becomes ritualized behavior, and this kind of morality is a dried husk, empty of actual virtue, and eventually causes trouble.

Life lived as an expression of *de* does not pedantically follow rules or conventions. Imagine doing good without keeping mental records of who did what for whom. True virtue helps without the motive of gaining merit; it acts without a sense of self. This goes against our common conditioning, but "the luminous Way seems dull" to worldly eyes, it seems to retreat even if it is in fact the only real progress. The way of the highest virtue will often look deficient, flimsy, or uncertain, but this is because we do not yet recognize the true nature of the Universe or whence virtue comes.

The sage is one who finds his or her life-force in *de*. He or she acts out of no other principle, and therefore acts in freedom, regardless of the actions of others. In leading others, the sage's virtue precludes having a mind mired in self-interest: her heart-mind is the heart-mind of the people. She treats those who are good with goodness, and those who are not good she also treats with goodness, because such is the nature of the true virtue.

tian zhi dao (heaven's way)

8
Heaven's Way in the World

Dao creates all things, but does not act as a Crowned Head of the Universe. This is no small distinction from the three religions that arose in the Middle East. Not only does the Universe live and function without authority, but proper behavior comes about spontaneously without any notion of it being *commanded* by divine decree. If right behavior, or the best way we can get along in this world, is without coercion by commandments or punishments, then this behavior would have to be deeply felt to be the wisest or most sensible way to live.

For one who perceives the Dao, even the following of societal rules of order is to externalize what should be inward. If peaceful and compassionate behavior does not arise "of itself," it is an empty husk, that is, insincere activity, confusing to the heart. This is the nature of hypocrisy. Authentic harmony cannot come by way of threat or legal authority. Imposed harmony is not real harmony; it is just a meddling which is able to produce imitation order. If we believe peace, compassion, and justice will never be natural to

humans, we settle for *imposed* order. That is our great mental obsta-
cle. True order can only come from the deepest, hidden part of us
that recognizes it is one center of the Whole. It may be hidden, but
it is there already because we are not really a separate process from
the Universe, the Dao, or its outworking *de*.

The Dao is the Way. It is also the Way of heaven enacted on
this earth. The life of the sage is one which has ceased asserting
things against the flow of Dao and instead flows with it, indeed,
becomes *identified with* it. So wisdom is here a process of observing
the natural flow of creation, and the recognition that asserting oneself against nature is absurd. D.T. Suzuki once made the following
observation about western religions: "God against man. Man against
God. Man against nature. Nature against man. Nature against God.
God against nature. Very funny religion!"[17] These false antagonisms
disappear when the cosmology is not based on concepts of a divine
monarch or judge wholly separate and above all in some adminis-
trative role. This is why the *Dao De Jing* does not introduce cosmic
authority or obedience to commandments.

Wherever our virtue relies on externals we are cultivating
hypocrisy. Hypocrisy is, after all, the making of an outward show
of actions for which there is insufficient inward correspondence.
If it is not going to be pretense, goodness *must* come from within,
from how one *actually thinks and feels* about something. And when
it does come from within, it will, of course, be natural and spontaneous. When it is one's own, one can do nothing else; no authority
is required. Actions founded on anxiety before external authorities
are, willy-nilly, hypocritical actions.

One is either in harmony with Dao, living by its virtue, *de*, which
is inherent in all things naturally, or one lives in existential conflict
with oneself by being at odds with What Is. At odds with What Is,
one resorts to bulldozers for pushing Nature around and bombs to
push other peoples around and perhaps some pharmaceuticals to
push one's own psyche around, in the futile attempt to bring everything under "control." But why try to dominate what brought us

---

17 Recounted by Joseph Campbell in an interview with Bill Moyers, in the
televised series, The Power of Myth.

forth, nurtures and sustains us? The Daoist does not feel distinct from Nature and thus feels no compulsion to control or change it. In this cosmology the whole Universe is *unitary* rather than divisive. In other words, what appears to be a multiplicity of "myriad things" is, subtly and implicitly, a unity. It is *one* organism, *alive* with *de*, and it is *you* too. The way to live happily is for one's own virtue to be nothing other than the virtue of the Dao.

Dao is the unity—the subtle unified energy bringing all things into being—and *de* is its power or outworking which nurtures and sustains creation. When this is also one's own virtue, there is nothing one needs to cling to, and no moral records to keep. The wise person does the good work, then steps away and forgets about it. What comes of it is not his concern. If the Dao doesn't sustain the work, it need not be sustained.

Trusting the Dao and living authentically

If the Dao gave birth to the heavens and the earth, out of which we too have emerged, we can trust the universal Way. "Dao gives birth to all things; its power nourishes them; matter gives them form... therefore all things revere Dao and honor its power, not for reward, but spontaneously." The Way "brings things to life and nurtures them, raises and completes them, shelters them and gives them rest, supports and protects them. Creating without possessing, acting without laying claim, raising without controlling– all this is *deep virtue*" (verse 51).

"Deep virtue" is subtle; it is simply present and there is no idea of controlling it. Its source is hidden. Is my virtue calculated to extract respect, to be recognized as "good," to lay claim on results? Or does it come from something hidden, and arise naturally? This question is really about whether my "virtue" is the same as the Dao's virtue. If it is, my way in this world will be nurturing without demanding, and acting without laying claim. Jesus made a similar point: "When you give alms, don't sound a trumpet, as the hypocrites do in places of worship and in the streets, so they may be praised by men. I tell you, they have received their reward. But when you give alms, don't even let your left hand know what your right hand is doing!"

In ourselves we may call it virtue; in its universal sense we may call it the Primal Virtue. But from where does this kind of authentic living arise? Not from dead adherence to a system or an ideology, nor by commandments, threats, guilt, or even discipline, but by *observation*. Observation? Yes. There is a "see for yourself" attitude because what Laozi advocates is observable in life and nature. There is no arguing about this kind of virtue, as argument does not free the mind.

De grows in the field of free observation, observation that is not filtered through our previous mental conditioning. When we really look and *see* it for ourselves we do not need external convincing. And what does not rely on externals cannot be uprooted. "Cultivate it in your self, and virtue will be genuine. Cultivate it in your family, and it overflows. Cultivate it in your community, and it becomes established. Cultivate it in a nation, and it is super-abundant. Cultivate it in all beneath Heaven, and it is all-pervasive" (verse 54).

The influence of the sage on the realm

The Virtue of the Dao was not just for one's personal life where she or he "attends to Heaven," but was also seen as the only successful way to govern politically. It was believed that if an empire was governed by a sage in harmony with Dao, the power of that harmony and well-being would be effective throughout the land. This was not through legislation, but by the power of the sage's inward cultivation of *de*. By "attending to Heaven" in the inward life the sage will successfully take care of the people. Such a one is a storehouse of Virtue to benefit the whole realm, giving it long life and enduring vision. Again we are reminded of the two historical examples in Chapter Five on *wu wei*, where we see two of Old China's most successful, peaceful, and prosperous eras were under rulers who honored the Dao and operated by *de*.[18]

If the operation of the supreme virtue is true on the cosmic level, it is suitable in all levels of the human realm. If *de* operates in one's life through *not* controlling, and in the Universe without utilizing authority, then it is suitable for the State to operate by the

---

18 See also *Tao, The Watercourse Way*, by Alan Watts and Al Chung-liang Huang, pp. 84-86.

same Virtue. Such a State would remain in balance and create a last-ing virtue. The proviso is that the ruler is a sage attuned to Dao. This wise and valuable leader is one who is outwardly governing the people by inwardly "attending to Heaven." In all affairs, the sage finds nothing is better than moderation, for one must be attuned from the start, and remain so through psychic harmony and balance for the necessary accumulation of virtue. To govern well assumes an abundant accumulation of virtue.

To the mind-heart that abides in the Universal Dao, the accu-mulation of virtue is said to be such that "nothing cannot be over-come." We don't ask this of candidates today. We only ask that they spin notions and rhetoric convincingly enough that their elaborate misrepresentations not insult us. We *expect* the office to go to the most ambitious and best-funded. But for the Daoist, only one self-less enough to abide in the boundless and operate from its virtue is fit to govern a country. "This is called having deep roots and sturdy trunk – the way to long life and enduring vision" (verse 59).

Even ruling a large State is then, ideally, a minor affair, like cooking a small fish: too much fussing and prodding destroys it. It suggests that the sage, by *not* meddling, can bring the realm into such harmony that neither ruler nor people harm each other, as all are relying on the same *de*.

The sage governs with equanimity and without force, caring for others rather than dominating them. The aim is cultivation of the inner rather than accumulation of the outer. One's sufficiency is found in letting go rather than claiming, yielding rather than forc-ing, giving rather than taking. This is the operating principle of the Universe; it is the way of *virtue*. One may question whether this is realistic in what some like to call a "dog eat dog" world in which we believe in survival of the fittest. Can we imagine a general trying to lead his army with the power of *Dao*? The Daoists did not limit virtue to civilian life. In verse 68 comes the counsel: "The most skill-ful military officer is never warlike; the most skillful fighter is never angry; the most skillful victor does not engage confrontation; the most skillful manager places himself below others. This is called the virtue of non-aggression. It is called utilizing the other's energy and blending it with heaven. There is no higher principle!"

This kind of virtue recognizes that enemies are enemies on the relative level and family on the ultimate level; they too are part of the indivisible Whole. Once a state is utterly destroyed it cannot be restored and once a person is killed he cannot be revived. So Sunzi said in *The Art of War* that the highest excellence is not in winning every battle; the highest excellence is *to conquer without fighting.* Likewise the thirty-first verse of the *Dao De Jing* decries weapons as "tools of misfortune" and admonishes that "To enjoy victory is to enjoy killing people," and that when many people are being killed, victory should be "with tears and mourning, like conducting a funeral for kin." Daoists felt that nonaggression follows heaven's model. Heaven overcomes without battling and completes its goals without moving.

By now we see a recurring pattern in the teachings about the Dao's outworking power. Great virtue is in the simple rather than the clever, in the flowing rather than the forced, in returning rather than the reaching outward, in what is natural rather than in what is contrived, in generosity rather than competitive self-interest. Can we live this way? I'd like to close with Laozi's answer:

My words are very easy to understand,
and very easy to practice.
Yet in the world few understand;
few put them into practice.

My words have an Ancestor;
my deeds have a Lord.
It's because people don't understand Them
that they don't understand me.

Because those who understand me are few,
I am more highly valued.
Behold the sage:
    Outwardly, dressed in peasant's cloth;
    inwardly, carrying priceless jade.

Bibliography and Recommended Reading

Blofeld, John (1985), *Taoism: The Road to Immortality*, Shambala, Boston

Chan, Alan K.L. (1991) *Two Visions of the Way: A Study of the Wang Pi and the Ho-shang Kung Commentaries on the Lao-Tzu*, State University of New York Press, New York

Chan, Wing-tsit. (1963) *The Way of Lao-Tzu*, The Bobbs-Merrill Company, Inc., New York

de Bary, Wm. Theodore, and Chan, Wing-tsit, and Watson, Burton (1960), *Sources of the Chinese Tradition*, Columbia University Press, New York

Henricks, Robert G. (1989), *Lao-Tzu te-Tao Ching: A New Translation Based on the Recently Discovered Ma-wang-tui Texts*, Ballantine Books, New York

Lau, D.C. (1994), *Lao-Tzu Tao te Ching*, Everyman's Library, Alfred A. Knoph, New York

Red Pine, (1996), *Lao-tzu's Taoteching: translated by Red Pine with selected commentaries of the past 2000 years*, Mercury House, San Francisco

Star, Jonathan (2001) *Tao te Ching: The Definitive Edition*, Jeremy P. Tarcher/Putnam, New York

Watts, Alan, and Huang, Al Chung-liang (1975), *Tao: The Watercourse Way*, Pantheon Books, New York

Watts, Alan (1997), *Taoism: Way Beyond Seeking – The Edited Transcripts*, Charles E. Tuttle Co., Inc., Boston

Made in the USA
Las Vegas, NV
18 March 2021